Sagas
of the
Norsemen

Sagas
of the
Norsemen

VIKING AND GERMAN MYTH

MYTH AND MANKIND

Sagas of the Norsemen: Viking and German Myth
Writers: Loren Auerbach (Gods of War and Destiny, Lords of
Fertility and Prosperity, Creation and the Doom of the Gods)
Jacqueline Simpson (The Viking and Germanic World, Triumph
of the Hero, The Nordic Legacy)
Consultant: Hilda Ellis Davidson

Created, edited and designed by
Duncan Baird Publishers
Castle House
75–76 Wells Street
London W1P 3RE

DUNCAN BAIRD PUBLISHERS
Managing Editor: Stephen Adamson
Managing Art Editor: Gabriella Le Grazie
Editor: Helen Cleary
Designers: Iona McGlashan, Christine Keilty
Picture Researcher: Julia Hanson
Artworks: Brent Linley
Map Artwork: Iona McGlashan
Artwork Borders: Iona McGlashan
Editorial Researcher: Helen Cleary
Editorial Assistant: Andrea Buzyn

TIME-LIFE BOOKS
Staff for SAGAS OF THE NORSEMEN: Viking and German Myth
Editorial Manager: Tony Allan
Design Consultant: Mary Staples
Editorial Production: Justina Cox

Published by Time-Life Books BV, Amsterdam

First Time-Life English language printing 1997

TIME-LIFE is a trademark of
Time Warner Inc, USA

ISBN 0 7054 3533 4

Colour separation by Colourscan, Singapore
Printed and bound by Milanostampa, SpA, Farigliano, Italy

Title page: An enigmatic scene from a Viking-Age land
memorial stone possibly depicting a story relating to Thor.
Contents page: An enamelled figure characteristic of Irish
craftsmanship dating from the first half of the 9th century AD.
It was found in a grave in Myklbostad in western Norway.

30 29 28 27 26 25 24 23 22 21 20 19 18 17 16 15 14 13 12 11 10 9 8 7 6 5 4 3

Contents

THE VIKING AND GERMANIC WORLD

During the summertime, in about AD834, an important funeral was held at Oseberg, on the Oslo Fjord in Norway. The local people were burying a rich and powerful woman, probably a queen, whose lavish burial goods, sealed beneath her grave mound, were to astonish the archaeologists who uncovered them in fine condition more than a thousand years later. Such discoveries offer precious clues to past beliefs in the northern world.

Like virtually all men and women of heathen Scandinavia, the Oseberg lady was buried in her clothing, surrounded by objects that testify to her high status. She and a female companion lay on cushioned beds inside a small wooden structure which stood on the deck of a slender, delicately-built ship, about fifteen metres long, its high-soaring prow curled like a coiling snake. The boat was a sign of wealth but it also had a symbolic function, as death was considered to be a voyage to the Underworld.

Carvings and objects found on the boat provide further insight into Viking beliefs. Wooden posts carved into fierce, snarling animal heads were probably included among the grave goods to scare away hostile spirits from the boat, and metal rattles, which hung from a horse's harness, would have had the same purpose. Cooking utensils found next to the corpse suggest that the lady was expected to feed herself during her long journey.

The Oseberg ship burial opens a window onto the culture of large areas of Europe, including Germany, England and Scandinavia, before they were converted to Christianity. By combining information from early writings and from archaeology, much can be learned about that vanished world. The picture that emerges is one of a lifestyle and a philosophy that once rivalled those of Greece and Rome in influence. And even today the names of leading figures from northern mythology, from Odin and Thor to Tannhaüser and the Valkyries, have not lost their power to excite the imagination.

Above, left: A silver pendant from Ostergötland in Sweden depicts a Vendel warrior, distinguished by his helmet with raised eyebrow guards (c.AD1000).

Opposite: A snow-capped mountain scene in Norway, with the Geiranger Fjord beneath. Such landscapes form the background to the myths of the Vikings.

7

The Germanic Peoples

The Anglo-Saxons and the Scandinavians were both branches of the Germanic peoples, one of the major groupings of related tribes in Europe during the Dark Ages. Centuries later, learned, sympathetic historians from medieval Iceland and Denmark recorded their own history.

The term "Germanic" was a collective name used by Emperor Julius Caesar, Tacitus, and other Romans to identify those of the barbarian tribes of central Europe who were not "Celts". Since both sets of tribes frequently moved from one territory to another in a complicated series of wars and migrations over several centuries, the distinction was not purely geographic. Although Caesar wrote of Celts living west of the Rhine and Germans east of it, this was at best a snapshot of the political situation in his time, and was probably inaccurate.

Each tribe, naturally, had its own name for itself, its own king and its own history; even after migrating to a new territory it often kept its original name. The tribes' movements were spread over many generations, but two aspects of their dispersal are fairly well documented. The first (*c.*200BC–AD200) was the conflict between certain tribes and Roman armies. The second, known as the Migration Age (AD400–800), was a large-scale movement of peoples that shaped the political map of post-Imperial Europe. One example among many indicates the scale of these migrations: the Goths moved from Sweden to north Germany in the first century BC, and divided into two groups, the Ostrogoths and Visigoths; by the fourth century AD the former dominated an area north of the Black Sea, while the latter were in Romania. Both were then dislodged by Huns, after which the Ostrogoths settled in Italy and the Visigoths in Spain.

The distinguishing feature of these tribes was their language. Germanic peoples were those who spoke the Germanic tongue, rather than idioms that were Celtic-, Slav- or Latin-based. By about the eighth century AD Germanic dialects had developed and divided into Dutch, Flemish, English, Danish, Swedish, Norwegian and Icelandic. The last four form a "North Germanic" or Scandinavian sub-group, rather different from the main "West Germanic" stock because they split off early from it. Despite these divergences, however, the myths and legends remained much the same in both groups.

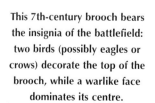

This 7th-century brooch bears the insignia of the battlefield: two birds (possibly eagles or crows) decorate the top of the brooch, while a warlike face dominates its centre.

If we try to trace the people's cultural identity to its origins by means of archaeological evidence, the picture becomes complex – not least because frequent migrations meant that the same territory was occupied by different peoples in succession, while trade contacts ensured that fashions in weapons and jewellery were not always reliable indications of tribal affiliation. However, the basic form of Germanic language was in use by about 500BC, and from then on Germanic culture existed alongside that of its territorial rivals, the Celts.

The situation during the Bronze Age (c.1500–c.500BC) is disputed. Rock carvings in southern Sweden prove the symbolic importance of ships, spears and axes, all of which were associated later with Viking gods. They also show evidence of agricultural rituals and sun worship which were not found subsequently. There are large votive offerings of war booty in Danish peat bogs dating from the Celtic Bronze Age and Iron Age. However, all this evidence may not be significant in terms of belief as it may just point to a preoccupation with weapons, ships and graves natural for any society in these periods of prehistory.

Our major sources of knowledge about Germanic heathenism, however, are not mysterious Bronze Age carvings or scraps of information from Roman writers, but the archaeology of the

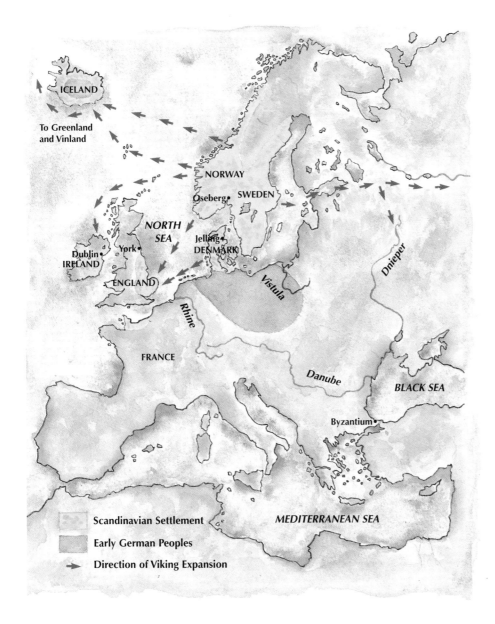

Map of Viking Expansion

The German-speaking peoples, made up of many tribes, originally populated that part of Europe enclosed by the rivers Rhine, Danube and Vistula. During and after the decline and collapse of the Roman Empire (c.AD200–600) they spread out in several directions, occupying areas as far south as northern Italy.

Scandinavian Settlement
Early German Peoples
Direction of Viking Expansion

Migration Age and Viking Age, together with heroic and mythic poetry and other written sources from the early Middle Ages. Most of these literary sources are Scandinavian, owing to the fact that this part of Europe was remote from the influence of Rome and did not become Christian until the tenth century – far later than England or southern and central Europe. Even after conversion, Icelandic and Danish writers preserved the myths and legends for their intrinsic interest.

Crucial to this preservation was the culture of the Vikings and their immediate descendants, notably the Icelanders. The term "Viking" does not, in fact, refer to a nation or territory, but to a way of life plundering foreign lands – it applied specifically to the seafaring Danes, Norwegians and Swedes who went raiding around the coasts of Europe, Ireland and Britain during the "Viking Age" (AD790–1050). However, the term can be loosely applied to all Scandinavians of this period, and also to every aspect of their culture.

The Vikings conducted the last of the great European migrations. Besides their raids, the Norwegians and Danes established permanent settlements in Normandy and England, controlled major trading towns in England and Ireland, colonized Iceland and Greenland, and briefly reached America early in the eleventh century. Meanwhile, Swedes spread along the Baltic shores, and their traders followed river routes across eastern Europe and Russia which led as far as Byzantium. Their travels brought them into contact with Muslims as well as Christians. Some of the former left coolly ironic accounts of the strange ways of these infidel traders, but Christian chroniclers were too censorious of their religious practices to discuss other aspects of heathen Nordic life.

Nevertheless, there were certainly peaceful contacts between the Vikings and neighbouring Christian lands, whose wealth, power and

Horsemen, common in Norse myth, are also represented in artefacts like this bronze monumental axe-head (*c.*700BC). Although axes and horned helmets are commonly associated with all the Vikings, they were actually only popular with the Danes and Norwegians.

prestigious learning must have been impressive to them. In the course of the ninth century this informal communication was supplemented by official religious missions strongly encouraged by the Christian rulers. One of these was led by the monk Anskar (later Archbishop of Hamburg), who was sent to Denmark and Sweden in AD829 and again in the AD840s by Emperor Louis the Pious. The descriptions of Anskar's journeys by his biographer Rimbert and in Adam of Bremen's *History of the Bishops of Hamburg* (*c.*AD1070) contain important information about Swedish festivals and sacrifices at the great temple at Uppsala.

Scandinavia was gradually converted by such missionary activity, coupled with the recognition of political advantage to be gained. The process was complete by AD1000 or shortly thereafter, except in Sweden, where heathenism maintained its hold for another two generations. With this notable exception the new faith seems to have been widely and easily accepted.

Witnesses from the Earth

Early Germans and Scandinavians worshipped in sacred places such as groves and islands, and seem to have used for their ceremonies only the simplest structures, which have left no archaeological traces. However, some sites have yielded other sorts of objects which provide some evidence of Germanic religious beliefs and practices.

Much of what we know of Viking religious practices comes from descriptions by travellers and missionaries. An Arab visitor in AD992 described markets on the Volga where Swedish merchants gathered, and said it was their custom to offer the gods food in a ring of tall posts carved with human faces. Another Arab, passing through the Jutland town of Hedeby in the AD950s, said its pagan inhabitants set up poles at their doors on which they hung the carcasses of sacrificed animals.

Accounts of the conversion of Northumbria in AD627, and of the Frisians and Franks in the eighth century, mention temple buildings containing wooden idols, while in the eleventh century there was a lavish temple at Uppsala, but little is now known about it.

Representations of gods and heroes were used decoratively as wall tapestries, on shields and on woodwork in fine houses. Unfortunately, most of these images have perished. However,

Runes

Runes are letters adapted from the alphabets current in Northern Italy about 200BC.

There were twenty-four letters in the original Germanic runic alphabet, but further letters were added to suit the languages of different areas.
    Runes are far more angular than their Italian originals, since they were used mostly on wood or stone, where straight lines are easier to cut than curves. The runic alphabet is called the "futhark", from the order of its first six letters: F, U, D (th), A, R, K.
    The characters had many practical uses, such as recording the maker's or owner's name on weapons and valuable objects, or for inscriptions on grave- and memorial stones.
    However, runes were also associated with magic, and the very word means "secret". Tacitus mentions symbols cut on wood and used in divination, while Icelandic sources often allude to runes used to heal, curse, give victory, calm storms, help in childbirth, or even to make the dead speak again.

A typical Germanic runestone, c.AD1000, now in the National Museum, Copenhagen.

11

some significant objects do survive: the Oseberg tapestry depicting a wagon; a series of tall carved and painted memorial stones from the island of Gotland off Sweden; and various helmets, especially those from Vendel in Sweden and Sutton Hoo in England. Sometimes it is possible to match the scenes shown on these objects with myths and hero tales from written sources – an eight-legged horse and its rider shown approaching a building on a Gotland stone must be Sleipnir carrying either Odin or a dead hero to Valhalla. But there are many other scenes and recurrent motifs whose interpretation can now only be tentative.

Intriguing images decorated helmets to give their wearers magic protection in battle. A common motif is the figure of a man wearing a horned helmet, sometimes clothed but more often naked except for a belt, and holding weapons; his legs are bent, as if leaping or dancing. These figures are reminiscent both of a German dance Tacitus describes, in which "naked youths leap and bound between upturned spears", and of the ferocious Berserks who fought naked and were inspired by Odin (see page 35). Other helmets show a warrior subduing a monster.

By far the most popular amulet in the later part of the Viking Age was a miniature hammer (the symbol of Thor) that was worn as a pendant. More than forty have been found. Thor was a protector of humanity against evil forces, not a war god, a point borne out by the fact that the little hammers have been found in women's graves as

TIME LINE Viking/Germanic History	AD100–400	AD400–500	AD500–600	AD600–800
Although the mythology of the North goes back to the Scandinavian Bronze Age (1500–500BC), the zenith of Germanic and Viking culture falls within the period that begins with the departure of the Romans (c.AD200) and ends with the Christianization of Scandinavia around 1000–1100AD.	c.100 Tacitus identifies Germanic tribes 375 Death of Ermanaric		526 Death of Theodoric 568 Langobard kingdom established in Lombardy 573 Death of Alboin of Lombardy 597 Conversion of England begins	

A late Bronze-Age figurine from Denmark of a woman holding a bowl.

A 5th-century memorial stone from Gotland.

c.400 Anglo-Saxons begin to colonize Britain
436 Death of Gundaharius (Gunther, Gunnar) of Burgundy
453 Death of Attila (Etzel, Atli) the Hun
474 Theodoric (Dietrich) becomes King of the Ostrogoths

A 6th-century helmet, found at Sutton Hoo, UK, but made in Denmark.

An 8th-century church stave from Helgö in Sweden.

c.750 Beowulf composed
772–82 Conquest and conversion of the Saxons by Charlemagne
790s Viking raids in western Europe and Britain.

A Viking-Age bronze spear with a decorated silver hilt. The Germanic tribes were often in conflict with one another and warfare was pivotal to their survival. The spear was common in eastern Scandinavia, while the sword was favoured in the south.

well as those of men. Another frequently found symbol is that of a woman holding out a beaker or horn; the figure is presumed to be that of a Valkyrie welcoming a dead hero to Valhalla.

Archaeology is also the prime source of our knowledge about pagan funerary rites. In burial, the body, dressed and accompanied by tools and weapons, might be laid directly in the ground, or put in a coffin or a wooden chamber, or, most dramatically, in a ship, as at Oseberg; the grave might or might not be covered with a stone cairn or earth mound. Cremations could be equally lavish, but little evidence survives from them as the dead men's possessions were usually also burned on the pyre.

In sharp contrast to these honorary funerals, one occasionally finds corpses treated with deliberate contempt. Bodies have been found buried face down, or with the head cut off and laid between the legs. There are several examples of both these types in Anglo-Saxon cemeteries. Some of the victims seem to have been killed by beheading, while others were decapitated after death, presumably to prevent the body turning into one of the malevolent "Undead" (see pages 102–103). Finally, some sacrificial victims were buried in bogs, which preserved objects with surprising effectiveness (see pages 122–23).

AD800–900		AD900–1000	AD1000–1100	AD1100–1300
c.800 German *Lay of Hildibrand* composed **820s** Anskar's first missionary journeys to Denmark and to Birka, Sweden **c.834** Oseberg ship burial, Norway **845** Viking raid on Paris led by Reginar (Ragnar Lodbrok) **c.870–940** Harald Fairhair, King of Norway	**876–879** Vikings settle permanently in England **c.860** Norse settlement in the Faeroe Islands **c.870–930** Norse settlement of Iceland	**930** Foundation of the Icelandic Althing (General Assembly) **c.950–960** Denmark converted to Christianity **c.950** Some of the *Poetic Edda* composed. **c.960** Harald Bluetooth, King of Denmark, converted to Christianity **c.964–1000** Olaf Tryggvason, King of Norway, converted to Christianity **c.986** First Viking expedition to North America **c.995–1022** Olaf Skotkonung, King of Sweden, converted to Christianity; establishment of Bishopric at Skara	**1100–1200** Stave churches built in Norway **c.1215** Saxo's *History of the Danes* **c.1220** Snorri's *Edda* **c.1230** *Niebelungenlied* composed

A Viking brooch (c.1050).

c.1000 Iceland converted to Christianity
1016 Conversion of Norway
1019–1035 Cnut the Great, King of Denmark
1030 Battle of Stiklestad and death of Olaf Haraldsson, later St Olaf
1042–1047 Magnus unites Norway and Denmark
1070 Adam of Bremen's *History of the Bishops of Hamburg*

The prow of the Oseberg ship in which a woman of status was buried in the 9th century.

12th-century ivory chessmen carved in western Norway.

Heroic Poetry

Although the Germanic and Scandinavian peoples developed an alphabet during pagan times, they mainly used it for brief inscriptions; surviving literary and mythological texts were all written down by Christians, using the Roman alphabet. These texts are the final phase of a long tradition of oral poetry, song and storytelling that preserved ancient tales of gods and heroes.

The earliest witness to the oral art of the Germans is Tacitus, who mentions in his *Annals* (written *c.*AD114) that a German tribe called the Cherusci were still singing lays about Arminius, a leader of theirs who had become famous almost a century earlier for wiping out three Roman legions encamped in the Teutoberg Forest. Various historical figures of the Migration Age such as Ermanaric the Goth (*d.*375), Attila the Hun (*d.*453), Gunther the Burgundian (*d.*436), and Theodoric the Ostrogoth (*d.*526) reappear centuries later as heroes and villains in the poetry of Germany, Anglo-Saxon England and Iceland, so stories about them must have been passed down orally for many generations.

Oral storytelling tends to simplify, personalize and dramatize the facts it transmits, while enhancing their emotional impact. A good example is the story of Ermanaric's death. A Roman contemporary records that he killed himself in terror when the Huns attacked his empire, but by the mid-sixth century the historian Jordanes in his *History of the Goths* described the episode instead as a dramatic tale of vengeance. To punish some rebellious subjects, he claimed, Ermanaric captured their chieftain's wife, Sunhilda, and had her torn to pieces by

A detail of an illustration from a manuscript collection of the Icelandic sagas – one of our principal sources for everyday beliefs about the Norse gods and the world they inhabited.

wild horses; her brothers subsequently wounded him so severely that he was too sick to resist an attack by the Huns soon after. Ninth-century Norwegian and Icelandic poems show the next stages in the embellishment of the story, in which the murdered woman has become the king's own wife, falsely accused of adultery, and the vengeance of her brothers, though successful, costs them their lives. Later, Sunhilda and her brothers are linked to two famous heroic families called the Volsungs and the Burgundians. Finally, as an explanation of Ermanaric's cruelty, medieval poems and sagas give him an evil counsellor (himself motivated by revenge) whose lies trick him into murdering all those who had once been close to him. The great legends of the Volsungs, the downfall of the Nibelungs, the death of Attila and other examples evolved in a similiar way.

The Norse poems that have survived are of several types. The simplest in style are those in the *Poetic Edda*, a collection of anonymous lays about gods and heroes found in a single Icelandic manuscript of about 1270, but mostly composed about 300 years earlier, before the country became Christian. The length of the lays range from 200 to 1000 short lines. Some are question-and-answer poems on mythological topics; others are narratives about gods or heroes, written in a swift-moving style.

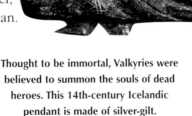

Thought to be immortal, Valkyries were believed to summon the souls of dead heroes. This 14th-century Icelandic pendant is made of silver-gilt.

They are a primary source for the myths concerning the fights of Thor against giants, Odin as the lord of wisdom, magic and poetry, the death of Balder, the wooing of Gerd by Freyr, the creation and destruction of the world, and Loki the troublemaker. The main heroic legends included are the life and death of Sigurd the Volsung, and the deaths of Gunnar and Hogni (see pages 90–92 and 95). The *Poetic Edda* also contains poems about another Volsung named Helgi and the Valkyrie who protected and married him; about Volund (Wayland) the Smith; and about Ermanaric.

It should be noted that the Eddaic poems are composed about, not to, the gods – they are not hymns or prayers. No doubt such things existed, but none survive, unless one counts a fragmentary poem of the late tenth century addressed to Thor and listing ghouls he had slain: "You struck Starkad down,/ You trampled on dead Gjalp ... ". Two charms have survived that invoke Wodan as a healer, one in Anglo-Saxon against snakebite, and one in Old German against a dislocated limb; also extant is an Anglo-Saxon invocation to the "mother of the earth" to bless the fields, addressing her by the otherwise unknown name "Erce". Apart from these small items, no cultic verse remains.

Norway and Iceland produced many "scaldic" verses, composed from the ninth century onwards, generally by poets at a king's court, celebrating his victories and generosity. Scaldic poems are not narratives, but short, ornate stanzas of praise; they often use brief, ingenious allusions to myths and legends as literary decoration. Their authors can usually be identified and dated.

Another form of narrative verse, more leisurely and solemn than the Edda lays, was the epic. Unfortunately, only one complete example survives, the English *Beowulf*, probably composed in the eighth century to entertain an aristocratic Christian audience with heroic pagan legends from their ancestral homelands. Germany also had epics at this period, but only a fragment of one remains: the tragic tale of Hildibrand and Hadubrand (see pages 105–106). None have survived from Scandinavia.

Lost Gods and Goddesses

Information about pagan deities in the Migration and the Viking Ages largely reflects the prestige of warfare among kings and warriors. The religious preoccupations of farmers, merchants and women at those times and earlier have to be gleaned from a few tantalizing fragments.

Bronze Age rock carvings in Sweden and Norway include representations of men ploughing, animals, sexual intercourse, ships on which men are dancing, leaping, or blowing horns, and ships carrying trees. There are warlike figures too – men brandishing axes or spears, and others holding up huge (possibly ceremonial) weapons. However, the dominant theme of these carvings is the journey of the sun, a vital matter to farmers and stockbreeders so far north, and many of the carvings are of large disks which seem to be sun symbols, held aloft by men or carried on ships. Further evidence of the importance of the sun to these early peoples is a metal figurine from Bronze Age Denmark, which consists of a golden sun disk on a horse-drawn chariot, perhaps a model of a life-size original (see pages 118–19).

The names of two early goddesses have survived: Nerthus, whom Tacitus also calls "Mother Earth", and who was worshipped by Danish tribes, and Nehalennia, whose shrine was on the Dutch islands of Walcheren and Noord-Beveland, where Roman-style altars and inscribed stones were set up by merchants and seafarers in the third century AD. The goddess is shown with fruit, a dog, or a ship. Both Nehalennia and Nerthus were associated with safety and prosperity, and were honoured by men as well as by women. Some Anglo-Saxons also worshipped a goddess called Rheda, to whom sacrifices were offered in March, and another called Eostre, whose festival was in April (and who gives us our word "Easter"); nothing more is known of either deity.

Other female deities were worshipped in groups, not as individuals. Most notable of these are the "Mothers", to whom there are many Roman-style monuments along the Lower Rhine and in areas where Germanic units of the Roman army were based (*c.*AD100–500). They are often shown in threes, holding fruit, loaves or infants, and appear to be guardians and givers of good fortune. In England, the Angles celebrated New Year's Eve as "the Night of the Mothers". Such groupings of goddesses foreshadow the Norns, Valkyries and guardian spirits of much later Icelandic texts, and hint that female divinities had once played a more prominent part in communal religion than surviving texts indicate.

Early goddesses were often shown in threes, bearing fruit.

Medieval Literature

Two important collections of Norse mythology were compiled almost concurrently at the beginning of the thirteenth century: *The History of the Danes* by the Danish historian Saxo Grammaticus (*c.*1215), and the *Prose Edda* of the Icelander Snorri Sturluson (*c.*1220).

Saxo Grammaticus was a cleric who wrote a history of the Danish nation in Latin. Its first nine books deal with legendary persons and events, and draw heavily on heroic lays that are now lost and on oral stories. Using both Danish material, as in the story of Bjarki (see pages 82–83), and tales given him by Norwegians and Icelanders, Saxo was mainly concerned with human kings and heroes. He also mentioned gods, but it was always with hatred and contempt, because he held puritanical and intolerant religious attitudes.

Snorri Sturluson's personality was very different, and his *Edda* is the liveliest, most comprehensive and most attractive account of Nordic myth and legend. He was a rich Icelandic landowner and local chieftain, expert in law and active in public life. We know that in 1218 he visited the Norwegian court, where he was granted feudal titles. Snorri was a poet in the scaldic style of ornate praise-poetry, technically skilful but somewhat dry, and he wrote a lengthy history of Norway in terms of the kings' lives, for which scaldic poems were an essential source. But he realized that many of his contemporaries found these old works difficult to understand, and so composed his *Edda*, which is at the same time a handbook on the rules of style and metre and a manual on Scandinavian mythology.

One of the main features of scaldic poetry is its "kennings", in which some common word such as "king", "ship" or "gold" is avoided, and replaced by a figurative expression which often involves an allusion to mythology. Thus, as Odin was the god of war, any battle could be called "Odin's storm", and for the sake of variety or metrical convenience any of Odin's numerous names could be used – one could, for example, say "storm of the

A Viking-style boat decorates a 14th-century illuminated manuscript of Snorri Sturluson's *Prose Edda*. The *Edda* is generally held to be the most energetic and accessible account of Nordic myth and legend.

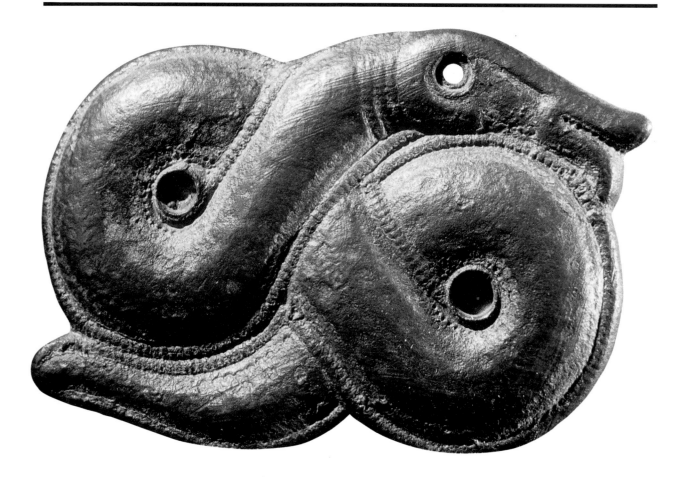

Jormungand, the snake who was one of the greatest enemies of the gods – especially Thor – grew so large that it wrapped itself around the world. This 7th-century brooch from Öland in Sweden possibly represents the world serpent.

Gallows-Burden", referring to his hanging on Yggdrasil (see page 31). Hero legends provide material too; because Sigurd won the pile of gold on which the dragon Fafnir lay, and carried it away on his horse Grani, gold could be referred to as "Fafnir's bed" or "Grani's burden". The knowledge of pagan tradition (necessary to compose, or even to understand, such kennings) had survived christianization in Iceland, but Snorri feared it would quickly be forgotten. The *Prose Edda* is his response to the danger of such a loss.

He therefore supplies a systematic survey of the main myths, beginning with creation myths, passing on to the attributes and adventures of the various gods and goddesses, and finally foretelling the death of Balder, the doom of the gods and the destruction of the world. This well-constructed narrative is followed by a section built around specific questions about mythological allusions in poetry, with a profusion of examples. Many details of mythology are recorded here, as are legends about Germanic heroes.

Snorri's knowledge is drawn chiefly from the same sources as were to be used by the *Poetic Edda*, plus scaldic verses and oral tradition. Several of his best stories are not known from any other source, and without his comments and explanations much scaldic poetry would have become incomprehensible. It is quite possible that the very fact that the ancient lays of gods and heroes were collected in the manuscript now called the *Poetic Edda* is due to Snorri's interest in such matters some fifty years before. If so, the debt we owe him is incalculable.

Other Sources

From the thirteenth century onwards, European taste turned increasingly towards new heroes and a new literary style: long, loosely-plotted adventure stories about the Knights of the Round Table or the peers of Charlemagne, which usually ended happily. Some of the more fantastic elements of Germanic belief were adapted to the new genre; giants, dwarfs, dragons, elves, magical weapons and rings could all fit into a romance about chivalry as easily as into a heroic lay. But in most Nordic countries the ancient heroes and pagan gods were forgotten.

Germany was the main exception. There, thirteenth century poets reworked old stories about early figures such as Dietrich, Hildibrand, Gunther, Walter or Etzel (Attila) the Hun. The supreme execution in this style was the *Nibelungenlied*, which retells the story of Siegfried (Sigurd the Volsung), powerfully mingling harsh tragedy with strong pathos and courtly elegance (see pages 92–95).

In Iceland, a major new art form appeared at this time – the saga. Sagas were substantial prose works which might be described as historical novels based on communal tradition. Some, the "Family Sagas", described the lives of early Icelandic settlers and their descendants in the tenth and eleventh centuries. These sometimes include references to pagan practices; for instance, that one man worshipped Freyr, and kept a fine stallion sacred to him. They also have a great deal to say about ghosts, magic and witchcraft. Although written from a Christian angle, the Family Sagas preserve the ideals of the pagan heroic age by their stress on honour, the duty of revenge, and the importance of meeting death with courage.

The other major group, the "Sagas of Ancient Times", are concerned with legendary Norwegian or Danish heroes of the Migration Age and Viking Age. These are vigorous, exciting tales, based on old poems and chronicles but retold in a simpler style than their originals. Their authors would skilfully weave many sources into a continuous narrative. Thus, the *Volsunga Saga* harmonizes numerous poems and traditions about Sigurd and associated figures into one long, tragic tale; another saga deals with Bjarki and King Hrolf whom he served; another gathers together German material about Dietrich and his champions. Various gods and goddesses feature in these works, especially Odin, whose function as the giver of victory or of death in battle is obviously relevant.

By careful assessment of all these various sources, scholars have pieced together a picture of the beliefs and tales of Germanic peoples. No doubt much is lost, but enough remains to give us some understanding of a major period in cultural history.

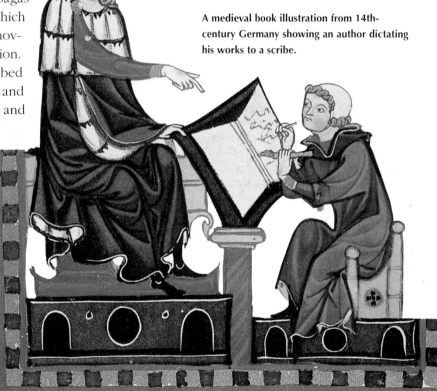

A medieval book illustration from 14th-century Germany showing an author dictating his works to a scribe.

THE OSEBERG SHIP BURIAL

Aparticularly sumptuous ship burial, dating from the ninth century and seemingly connected with a fertility cult, was excavated in 1904 at Oseberg in southern Norway. Two women were found in the grave, one of high rank, possibly a priestess of the Vanir, and an attendant, together with a multitude of precious, elaborate objects. Corn, nuts, seeds and apples were also found. The peat soil of the burial place had preserved the ship and its contents well, although the grave had been raided not long after its completion. It contains a wonderful, if enigmatic, record of Viking beliefs.

The burial ship contained an exquisitely carved small wagon (*right*), of the type that was used to carry a fertility god or goddess around the country to visit communities and bless the season. The wagon itself was decorated on all sides with mysterious human and animal figures, possibly illustrating mythological scenes. Fantastic figures were also found on other objects, such as this monstrous head (*below*) from one of four carved wooden sledges found in the grave.

Above: The Oseberg ship, which can now be seen in the Viking Ship Museum in Oslo, was a large and beautiful pleasure craft not suitable for the open sea. A burial chamber was built centrally, behind the mast, and the ship was found moored within the burial mound by a large stone in its centre.

Below: The restored prow of the Oseberg ship shows intricate carving. The prow was badly damaged by raiders who broke into the grave shortly after the burial. The malicious damage they caused suggests fear and hatred of those buried, rather than robbery.

Above: Another monstrous head of an animal found in the ship. There were five such heads, thought to have been carved by the same hands that worked the wooden sledges. They had no practical use, and must have been symbolic.

Left: This impressive ship, from another ship burial in Gokstad, Norway, was seaworthy, unlike the Oseberg ship. The Gokstad craft is a fine example of the extraordinary Viking ships, which fused proportion, skilled construction and efficiency in perfect harmony.

GODS OF WAR
AND DESTINY

The main group of Norse gods, known as the Aesir, are recognizably human, dominated by the cunning Odin, supreme divinity, and the sometimes brutish Thor, god of thunder and ruler of the sky. Colourful in their foibles, and always eager to feast and carouse, they conspire and compete with each other and their enemies in a series of vivid episodes. Accompanying them is the wily Loki, who, although not divine, lived among the gods and often caused a distinctly earthly kind of mischief.

The stories of the gods are played out against a setting that also resembles the human world. Stamina and endeavour were necessary to survive the harsh environment inhabited by the Germanic peoples, and similarly a tough sensibility pervades the ice-bound mountain fastnesses of the Norse imagination. The myths mirror a human sphere dominated by climate and terrain, and tell of menacing elemental forces against which the gods must pit their wits and strength.

Formidable giants posed a particular threat to the gods, providing a constant supply of fearsome enemies. The relationship between gods and giants was not merely combative; many of the gods had affairs with giantesses, even sometimes marrying them, and Odin himself was said to be descended from a giant. Usually, however, these races were at odds with each other. It was understood by all in the divine realm that giants had to be subdued, which usually culminated in their receiving a crushing blow from Thor's hammer.

The harsh landscapes of Northern Europe, which experienced just a few frost-bitten hours of daylight between long winter nights, provided more than just a mythical setting. In such a region, where the determination to survive was tested by pitiless weather conditions and tribal violence, it was hardly surprising that the Norse people had an intense awareness of fate. Without remorse Odin selected those who were to die in battle, and an apocalyptic demise, even for the gods, was inevitable. In the divine realm all roads led to Ragnarok – the end of the world.

Above, left: **Found at a boat burial in Vendel, Sweden, this elaborate 7th-century helmet is forged in iron and embellished with bronze. It was discovered with a hoard of fine weapons, all of the highest quality.**

Opposite: **The threatening Midgard serpent dominates this 17th-century manuscript which also depicts Valhalla, the realm of the gods found above and beyond the mortal world.**

23

The Aesir

The Norse gods lived together in the realm called Asgard, beyond and above the human world. Here they held heated debates about their various dilemmas – how to regain hostages from the giants, how to deal with the evil progeny of Loki, how to protect their magical treasures. They interacted with each other like any other social group, and were characterized by superhuman strength rather than by moral absolutes.

Asgard was originally inhabited by the Aesir alone. Another tribe of gods, known as the Vanir, coexisted with them in the realm of Vanaheim. But the two groups fought a long, bloody war, after which a few members of the Vanir came to live in Asgard.

Little is known of this war, but we are told that the most important of the Vanir who came to Asgard were Njord, god of the sea, and his twin children: the god Freyr and the goddess Freyja. Whereas the Vanir were deities of fertility, presiding over land and sea, the Aesir were associated with war, magic and the sky. The magician Odin was their chief and Thor, protector of Asgard, was second-in-command. Adam of Bremen, an eleventh-century historian, reported that Odin made wars and blessed men with bravery in battle, while Thor ruled in the sky, governing thunder, lightning, the winds and the rain.

The Icelandic chronicler, Snorri, tells that all the other Aesir, mighty as they were, deferred to

These three standing figures from a woven tapestry of *c.*1100 have been identified as the trio of primary gods worshipped by the Norse people – Odin, Thor and Freyr. Odin, with one eye, stands on the left wielding not a spear but an axe, while the central figure gripping a hammer is probably Thor. The third figure holds an ear of corn or a piece of fruit – symbols of Freyr's role as a fertility god.

Sacred Places

The Norse deities were not always worshipped in elaborate temples and holy buildings. Sites of natural beauty were sometimes chosen as idyllic settings in which to venerate the gods and frequently they were not even marked by a monument.

This beautiful lake at Thingvellir in Iceland was probably held to be sacred since the island's "Althing" (an annual assembly of free men) met nearby in the Viking Age.

The Roman historian Tacitus described how the Germans did not confine their worship to a domestic forum, but also consecrated open forests and groves. Many Scandinavians, particularly those who settled in Iceland, also chose natural venues as their sites of worship. Literary sources tell of sacrifices brought to groves, rocks and stones, which were believed to represent patron gods. In the poem *Hyndluljod*, Freyja tells how her favourite human, Ottar, set up a cairn in her honour.

Sacred places might be chosen for their outstanding beauty. One such site, Helgafell (Holy Mountain) in Snaefellsness, Western Iceland, is mentioned in the *Eyrbyggja Saga*. Thorolf Mostur-Beard, a devoted follower of Thor who emigrated to Iceland, held this mountain to be so sacred that no one was even allowed to look at it if they were unwashed, and no living creature, man nor beast, was to be harmed there.

The same Thorolf also held sacred the place where the pillars of his high seat (removed from a previous site and brought on the journey) had washed ashore (see page 38). Thorolf gave orders that it should not be desecrated with either bloodshed or excrement. The latter taboo was in conflict with the Icelandic custom of groups urinating on the grass at the end of meetings.

Unsurprisingly, the site was desecrated after Thorolf's death – following an assembly a rival family declared that they were going to follow the normal custom and urinate there. Thorolf's son and his men attacked them for this affront; a fierce fight ensued, with blood spilt on both sides, defiling the holy ground even further. After this, the temple and the assembly were removed to a fresh venue.

The bridge between Asgard and Midgard, the immortal and mortal worlds, was called "Bifrost". Snorri describes it as the rainbow, consisting of three plaited strands of fire.

Odin like children to their father. Odin was a formidable and frightening character, rather less concerned with the protection of his subjects than with the accumulation and exercise of his own magical powers.

Odin's wife was Frigg, who, like him, was credited with the ability to foresee the future. She was queen of the gods and first lady among the goddesses. Stately, gracious and bountiful, she also had a maternal aspect accentuated by her concern for her son, Balder. In this capacity she was invoked by women during childbirth and by those wishing to conceive. Frigg and Odin's other children included Hod, who was to play an unwitting role in Balder's fate, and Hermod, who was to prove himself in an act of outstanding bravery (see page 126).

Many of the gods were actually said to be the offspring of Odin. Thor was his eldest son, although not by Frigg. Thor's mother was Jord (Earth), with whom Odin had an extra-marital liaison. Thor in turn was married to Sif, a beautiful golden-haired goddess, although he also had two sons, Modi and Magni, by a giantess, Jarnsaxa.

The Realm of the Gods

The Norse people envisaged a world divided into three different levels, one above the other. Asgard, realm of the gods, lay above Midgard, the world of men surrounded by vast oceans. Beneath Midgard was Niflheim, the land of the dead presided over by Loki's gargantuan daughter, Hel, who gave her name to the realm's citadel.

It was in Asgard that the gods had their magnificent homes. Odin's two halls were called Valhalla, hall of the slain, and Valaskjalf, which contained his high seat Hlidskjalf. Sitting on Hlidskjalf Odin could preside over the whole world, with a view of each level and all that went on in it, and only he and his wife, Frigg, were allowed this high privilege. Thor's hall, known as Bilskirnir, in the region of Thrudvangar, was said to be the largest building ever constructed, while there was no more beautiful place than Balder's hall, Briedablik, except perhaps the hall Gimli, which stood at the southernmost edge of the realm. Gimli was considered to shine more brightly than the sun, and it was believed that this building would remain standing after the end of the world. Gods were to live there at peace with one another after Ragnarok.

Also on this top level of the world were Vanaheim, home of the Vanir, and Alfheim, realm of the light-elves. Midgard, on the level beneath Asgard, was not only home to humankind but also to the giants, who lived in Jotunheim. A flaming bridge, Bifrost, of which Snorri says, "You must have seen it, possibly you call it the rainbow," was built between the two levels by the gods. The parts of the cosmos were also connected and sheltered by an ash tree, called the World Tree or Yggdrasill, which was an axis of the universe (see page 116).

Asgard was protected by a wall which was razed during the war against the Vanir, leaving the realm defenceless. A builder approached the Aesir and offered to construct a mighty barrier that would be completely secure against giants. In payment, he requested the goddess Freyja as his wife, and the sun and the moon for his own. The Aesir decided to agree to the builder's demands on condition that he complete the wall before summer – which gave him six months – but if it was at all unfinished on the first day of the new season they insisted that his price would be forfeit. They felt sure that he could not possibly finish such a task in that time, and they secretly hoped to gain the best part of a wall without cost. Furthermore no one was to aid him in the work. However, the builder asked that he might have the help of his stallion, Svadilfari and, ever-mischievous, Loki persuaded them to consent.

The Aesir were amazed at the size of the rocks that the stallion was able to pull, and the builder's work rate increased threefold with his assistance. As winter wore on, the team's progress continued apace and the wall rapidly became so high and strong that it could never be breached. Contrary to the Aesir's anticipation, the builder had almost completed his task a full three days before the alloted time.

Somewhat alarmed, the gods met to discuss tactics. They asked each other who had been responsible for this impetuous bargain which could end in the loss of Freyja, the sun and the moon. Blaming Loki for having persuaded them to agree to the use of the stallion, they seized him and told him to resolve their predicament. Loki promised to do so.

That night, when the builder went to fetch stone with Svadilfari, Loki, disguised as a mare, cantered out of the wood and drew near to the stallion, easily distracting him. As she ran away he raced off into the wood after her. All night the horses chased each other among the trees, leaving the hapless builder powerless to finish his work. Realizing now that he would not fulfil the Aesir's ultimatum, the builder flew into a monstrous rage. At this his guise slipped and the gods could see that he was in fact a giant. They called for Thor. He appeared immediately with his hammer raised to reward the giant not with Freyja, the sun and the moon, but with a smashed skull. Then the impostor was sent to Hel. Meanwhile, Loki, who had taken the mare's form, was to give birth to a magical horse called Sleipnir.

Picture stones such as this were first used in Gotland as monuments to the dead. This example, from the Germanic Iron Age, is incised with an image of the sun and vignettes of hunting.

Odin, God of War and Magic

Perhaps the most complex of all the Norse Gods was Odin. Presented in the sources as foremost of the Norse pantheon and known as "Allfather", he was not, however, a benevolent father-god – he was as fickle as he was powerful, as treacherous as he was generous, and although respected and worshipped, he was never entirely to be trusted.

The supreme deity Odin is depicted in a medieval manuscript with his two raven companions Hugin and Munnin. Hugin is believed to represent memory, whereas Munnin personifies thought. Each day Odin would send them out into the world and they would return bearing news of events. Odin is typically represented with only one eye and wearing a dark hat.

Odin cut a terrifying figure: one-eyed and wearing a dark wide-brimmed hat that cast a shadow over his face, he travelled as a mortal wanderer. As a god of magic, war and wisdom, he visited Midgard to distribute knowledge and victory in battle. He had many names which hint at his various roles, and the diversity and fickleness of his character. He was known as Allfather (*Alfodr*), but also as Father of the Slain (*Valfodr*), God of the Hanged (*Hangagud*), God of Prisoners (*Haptagud*) and God of Cargoes (*Farmagud*). Snorri lists another forty-nine names that Odin was reputed to have called himself, which also reflected aspects of his character. Among these were *Harr* ("the high one"), *Grimr* ("the masked one"), *Svipall* ("the capricious one"), *Hnikarr* ("the inflamer"), *Glapsvidir* ("swift tricker"), *Sigfodr* ("father of victory"), *Blindi* ("the blind one"), *Baleygr* ("shifty eyed"), *Gondlir* ("one with a magic staff"), *Vidurr* ("destroyer") and *Yggr* ("terror").

Odin was invoked by his followers for victory in battle, and to give or deny victory was within his power. But he could be faithless, suddenly turning against his favourites and causing their rapid downfall, and he was sometimes accused of awarding triumph unjustly. It was in his interest, as a god of war, to promote strife, and it was said that he sometimes boasted of being able to incite nobles against each other so that they would never be reconciled again.

Odin was a master of magic and went to great lengths to further his supernatural powers. He was said to have only one eye because he had pledged the other in payment for a drink from the well of Mimir, situated beneath a root of the World Tree.

Odin Wins the Mead of Poetry

When Odin wanted to take the mead of poetry from the giant Suttung and give it to the gods he had to call on all his powers of cunning and guile.

Disguised as Bolverk, Odin persuaded Baugi to bore through a mountain to help him gain the mead of poetry.

Disguised as a mortal and calling himself Bolverk ("evil-doer"), Odin took up lodgings with Suttung's brother, a giant called Baugi, who had owned nine slaves, all of whom Odin had ruthlessly murdered. He offered to do their work, and as his price requested a drink of Suttung's mead of inspiration. Although it was not in his authority to agree to such a request, Baugi yielded.

When winter arrived, and he had completed his work, Bolverk demanded his reward and so the two of them set off for Suttung's mountain home. When they arrived, Suttung flatly refused to take any part in Bolverk and Baugi's pact. So Bolverk found an auger (an instrument for boring), and ordered Baugi to bore a hole into the mountain, which he believed contained the mead.

When a tunnel had been created, Bolverk transformed himself into a snake and slid into it. There he discovered Gunnlod, Suttung's daughter who guarded the precious liquid. He lay with her for three nights, for which she granted him three tastes of the drink. He drained the pot called Odroerir with the first drink, and in the next two sips he emptied the two vats Bodn and Son.

Odin then turned himself into an eagle and escaped to Asgard. Furious, Suttung also took the shape of an eagle and followed in pursuit. When the Aesir saw Odin flying towards them they quickly placed special containers in the courtyard, so that as he flew overhead he could release the mead into them. Suttung, however, was so close behind his opponent that he caused Odin to spill a little of the mead of inspiration outside the walls of Asgard, and ever since that time any mortal who so wishes has been free to partake of it there.

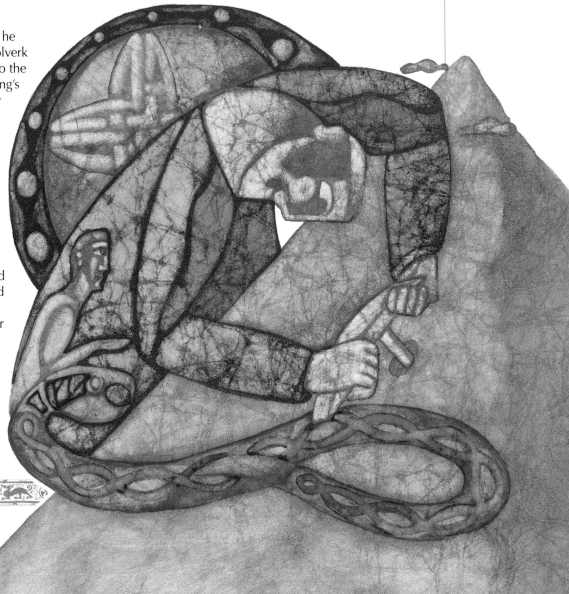

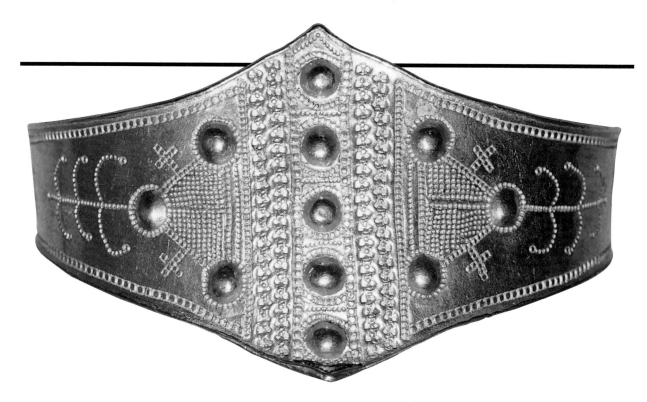

This golden armring (c.AD900) from Jutland in Denmark is elaborately decorated with a pattern symbolizing Yggdrasil, the Tree of Life. This giant ash tree was the axis of the Norse mythical world. Odin hung upon it for nine days and nights without sustenance in order to learn the secrets of the universe.

The water in this well promised inspiration and knowledge of the future to whoever drank it. Another version, however, claims that Odin gained wisdom and information from the head of one of the gods, Mimir, the oldest and wisest of the Aesir, which he kept for himself after it had been cut off by the Vanir (see page 59). He was able to consult the head whenever he desired knowledge.

Odin could also change his shape at will, often flying through the air in the form of an eagle, and his spirit could be instantly transported to distant lands as any other bird or creature, while his body lay as if asleep. His magical abilities made him a formidable opponent – with mere words he had the power to both calm or stir the sea, extinguish fires or change the course of the winds.

It was also said of Odin that he only spoke in verse, and that poetic ability and inspiration were gifts that he alone bestowed. For example, he blessed one of his favoured subjects, Starkad, with the ability to compose poetry as fast as he could physically speak the words.

The source of poetic inspiration was the mead of poetry, which Odin stole, to the benefit of humankind as well as himself. This magical liquid initially belonged to two dwarves. It came into being after the war between the Aesir and the Vanir (see page 24), when the two sides agreed to seal their truce by simultaneously spitting into a vat. The Aesir then took this spittle, which was a symbol of peace, and, not wishing to waste any amount, formed it into a man called Kvasir who was so wise that there was no question that he could not answer.

Kvasir travelled far and wide throughout the world imparting his knowledge to others until he eventually arrived at the home of the two malicious dwarves, Fjalar and Galar. They cunningly lured him into a private conversation so that they could kill him unwitnessed. Then they poured their victim's blood into two vats called Son and Bodn and a pot called Odroerir, before adding honey to create a rich mead. The resulting liquid conferred the ability to compose poetry or pronounce words of wisdom. To placate the gods who bemoaned the loss of their companion, the dwarves explained that Kvasir had suffocated in his own intelligence. However, they were not to keep the mead for very long as Odin took it from them for his own safeguarding.

Odin, the World Tree and Sacrifice

Although it would appear to be an important part of his story, the myth of Odin hanging on the World Tree survives only in one enigmatic passage from *Havamal* ("Words of the High One"). This tells how he underwent great suffering to win the runes, the source of wisdom and magical lore.

In the poem Odin himself narrates how he hung on a windswept tree identified as the World Tree, Yggdrasill, for nine full nights without food or water, slashed with a spear and sacrificed – "given to Odin, myself to myself" – until, screaming, he was able by virtue of his suffering to reach down and seize the magical runes. By this heroic deed Odin also learned nine magical songs from the son of the giant Bolthor and his wisdom became so great that he was able to master eighteen magical spells previously unknown to any man or woman.

There are obvious similarities between Odin's hanging on the World Tree and Jesus Christ's sacrifice on the cross: Christ hung on the Rood Tree, without food or water, and he was also pierced with a spear as was Odin. Christ cried out before dying as Odin cried out when he seized the runes during his self-sacrifice. Christian influence on *Havamal* cannot be entirely discounted, but crying out, hanging and stabbing are also ancient elements of Norse myth that are particular to the cult of Odin.

Lord of the Spear

Gungnir, Odin's spear, was specially crafted by the dwarves. It was his favourite weapon, and he used it to incite or reduce discord. Those who died by spear-wounds were sacred to Odin and went to serve him in Valhalla.

One of Odin's many epithets was "Lord of the Spear" and his own magical spear, Gungnir, was unstoppable in its flight.

Odin ruled over the point of no return – the moment at which the spear leaves the hand and cannot come back. An aspect of this was the initiation of war by the hurling of a spear above the opposing army. Sometimes it was said to be thrown by the war god himself, standing behind the host. Enemy armies could also be dedicated to Odin by flinging a spear over their heads, and if they fell they became an offering to him.

Those who were killed by a spear became part of the *Einherjar,* his troop of warriors in Asgard. Thus, human sacrifices to Odin were stabbed with a spear, ensuring that they would be received by him after death. A dying nobleman, free of battle-wounds, who wished to go to Valhalla instead of Hel (the citadel for those who died in their beds), could have himself lacerated with the point of a spear.

Odin with his spear and a raven confronts the wolf Fenrir on this panel from a Viking-Age cross on the Isle of Man.

31

Bodies that were sacrificed to Odin have been recovered from peat bogs hanged or killed with a spear (see page 31). Adam of Bremen, in his *History of the Archbishops of Hamburg-Bremen*, also describes the bodies of men and animals hanging in the trees near the temple at Uppsala, where a festival was held every nine years in honour of the gods. Prisoners of war who were killed as offerings to Odin were also often hanged.

Gautreks Saga has an account of a sacrifice to Odin involving one of the god's particular favourites, Starkad, whose destiny was shaped by the favour of Odin and the enmity of Thor. He was in the service of Vikar, the king of part of southern Norway, when the king's war-fleet lay becalmed near an island, and it was decided that the sailors must offer a human sacrifice to Odin to rouse a favourable wind. To everyone's horror, the lot of victim fell to King Vikar himself. That night Odin came to Starkad and led him into the forest to listen to a dispute with Thor concerning his own fate. Then Odin dismissed Starkad, saying that he expected repayment for the many favours he had shown him, and he wanted King Vikar in sacrifice. As Starkad left, Odin handed him a spear that appeared to be nothing more than a reed.

Next morning, Vikar's men decided that their best plan was to make a mock sacrifice of their king on the island, and Starkad offered to arrange it. He took a length of soft, raw calf-gut from the ship's cook and tied a noose in it, which he looped round Vikar's neck. He tied the other end to the slender twig of a sapling fir and made the king stand on a tree-stump; then he struck him in the chest with the reed, crying "Now I give you to Odin!" At once the stump rolled from beneath Vikar's feet, the reed became a spear, the gut a strong rope, and the twig a sturdy branch on which the king swung aloft to die a horrible death, simultaneously pierced and hanged.

Starkad had obeyed Odin, but at the cost of treachery which filled him with shame, especially because Vikar had been his lord and blood-brother, one of the most sacred bonds in the heroic code of honour.

Warriors killed by the spear were received by Odin in Valhalla. This Gotland memorial stone probably depicts Odin on his eight-legged horse, Sleipnir, hailing a dead soldier who will join his warrior group, the Einherjar, in Asgard.

Odin did not need food and lived on wine alone. He threw his portion of meat to the two wolves, Geri and Freki, who sat at his feet. Odin also had two ravens, Huginn and Muninn, whom he sent out every day over the world to bring him reports of happenings. In the evening they would sit on his shoulders and tell him about all that they had seen. Ravens are traditionally linked with battle and death, both poetically and in reality, as they were commonly found on the battlefield in the aftermath of war, scavenging among the corpses.

Odin's other animal was the extraordinary offspring of Loki and the stallion Svadilfari (see page 27). This creature, Sleipnir, had eight legs and was the fastest of all horses; he bore Odin through the sky at the head of the Einherjar. Sleipnir could leap the walls of Niflheim, and Odin used him for all his errands. The stallion was once lent to Hermod, who rode him to Hel in an attempt to save his brother Balder (see page 126).

Valhalla

In Valhalla each day the slain warriors put on their armour and ventured to the courtyard to fight one another. At dinnertime, all those who had fallen in the fighting rose again to sit together through the evening, carousing, feasting and drinking, at peace with the whole company.

The Einherjar were sustained by a never-ending supply of mead from the udder of Heidrun, a goat that stood on top of Valhalla, plucking and chewing leaves from a tree named Laerad. Every day she was milked to fill a vat so big that all the Einherjar could drink from it to repletion. Their food was the meat of the boar Saehrimnir, which was cooked daily in a special pot called Eldhrimnir and magically became whole again in the evening. The flesh of Saehrimnir was always sufficient to feed all the Einherjar, regardless of their number.

Those who were to join the ranks of the Einherjar were brought to Valhalla by special envoys, the Valkyries. These seem originally to have been ferocious female spirits who revelled in bloodshed and devoured victims on the battlefield. In some versions of myth there were only three Valkyries, all thought to live for ever, while in others there were twenty-seven, or thrice nine as the sagas put it, only a few of whom were thought to be immortal. Later in the Viking era they became more dignified and were portrayed as beautiful golden-haired female spirits who waited on the Einherjar in Valhalla, and went down to the battlefields both to grant victory according to Odin's decree and to lead the slain to Asgard.

Valkyries are of primary importance in the stories and poems about the legendary heroes (see page 90). Occasionally they are portrayed as supernatural beings of huge stature who snatched heroes from mortal danger. In other versions they were said to be protective spirits who blessed kings and princes who paid due respect to Odin, and received them as their husbands after the warriors' heroic deaths.

These two objects represent Hugin and Munin, Odin's two ravens, cast in the form of gilt and bronze harness mounts from Gotland, c.AD700.

33

From Wodan to Odin

Evidence suggests that the cult of Odin is very old. By the time of the Romans the Germans already had a protective deity, Wodan, who was invoked for success in battle, and also exhibited Odin's sinister and fickle nature. In pagan England, a god named Woden was patron of kings and princes and the god of war and magic.

The first-century Roman writer Tacitus describes a German god, Wodan, whom he identifies with the Roman god Mercury. He places him as the chief god of the Germanic peoples to whom human sacrifices were made. There has been little evidence found to differentiate this Wodan from the later Odin – he was god of the dead and of battles, and was associated with the spear, the wolf and the raven.

Understood to inspire his followers with a battle-frenzy, Wodan rendered them immune to fear or pain. He was also regarded as the primogenitor of kings, and received monarchs and nobles into his halls after death. Wodan was connected to trade and the economy: he was referred to in inscriptions as "Mercator" or "Negotiator", just as Odin was sometimes described as "god of cargoes".

In pagan England the Anglo-Saxons worshipped a god called Woden. The Anglo-Saxon royal dynasties looked upon Woden as their divine ancestor and traced their lineage to him. In certain genealogies Woden has a son named Baeldaeg, who has been identified with Odin's son Balder (see pages 124–127).

English place names with the meaning "Woden's barrow" suggest that Odin was originally associated with burial sites or mounds. Influenced later by the Scandinavian invaders, English homilists often used the Norse name Odin instead of Woden, which further attests to the link between the two gods.

The Capricious God of Kings

There are many stories in Saxo's sixteen-volume history of the Danes (see page 17) and in the heroic sagas (see page 19) which illustrate the volatile nature of Odin's support for his favourite kings, princes and nobles. He would give them weapons, yet it was thought that he could deliberately cause any of them to die unnecessarily so that the slain warrior would be forced to join the god's army in Valhalla and be available to support him at the final destruction of the world. Sigmund the Volsung, for example, received a magnificent sword which Odin himself had brought to the hall of King Volsung and thrust into the trunk of a tree that stood in the centre of the building. Yet during Sigmund's last battle Odin came onto the battlefield and fought against him, shattering the sword with his spear. This marked the end of Sigmund's run of good fortune; the battle turned against him and he was killed.

Odin also gave his followers valuable advice. He taught Sigmund battle spells, and he showed Hadding, another of his favoured followers, how to array his troops to give himself full advantage on the battlefield. And it was said that Odin himself stood behind Hadding's troops and shot ten arrows as one.

Odin appeared throughout Hadding's life, to rescue him, and to give him strength and spells to break his bonds when he was captured by enemies. He prophesied that he would never die at the hands of a foe but only by his own hand. Eventually the hero did hang himself – an appropriate death for a warrior who worshipped Odin.

It is told that Odin also taught the secret of arranging troops in a special formation to Harald Wartooth, King of the Danes, and pledged that he too would never be harmed by wounding. In return Harald promised Odin the souls of all those that he killed in battle. Odin granted the king victory for most of his life, but turned against him in his old age. In disguise, Odin bred enmity between Harald and his nephew, King Hring, and eventually caused a war. During this he betrayed the secret of Harald's battle formation to his enemy. When Harald realized that his opponent had anticipated the formation, he knew that only Odin could have imparted it, and that the god had deserted him. Finally, as he drove across the battlefield, he became aware that Odin had taken the place of his charioteer. He begged him for one more victory, but Odin paid no heed to his pleas, threw him from the chariot and slew him.

It was not only technical skill and resourcefulness in warfare that protected Odin's favoured armies from defeat – the god's magic also played a part. No human to whom he was opposed had the capacity to combat his cunning. Odin was able to blind, deafen, paralyze or strike panic into entire enemy armies and to blunt their weapons so that they were redundant. On the other hand, he was able to increase the strength of favoured armies and make them impervious to wounding.

Inspired by Odin a group of warriors known as Berserks would fight naked in a maddened state, unaffected by fire or weapons. Familiar historical figures in Norse literature, they served famous kings (such as King Harald Fairhair of Norway and King Hrolf of Denmark) as elite bodyguards, or roamed freely, seeking trouble either alone or in groups. In *Heimskringla* Snorri describes how these men went into battle as wild as dogs or wolves. They bit their shields and were as strong as the most ferocious bears or bulls.

This mould, found at Torslunda on the island of Öland in the Baltic, would have been used for making helmet plates. The figures were probably intended to bring luck in battle – the dancing youth in the horned helmet is thought to be a follower of Odin and the animal-like warrior may well represent a ferocious Berserk. It dates from the 6th century AD.

Thor, God of Thunder

Thor was the best-loved of the Viking pantheon. A mighty figure with colossal strength, a huge red beard and thick brows over glowering eyes, he strode about the cosmos, fighting giants and trolls. He was the protector of Asgard and the gods could always call upon him if they were in trouble. Life was simple for Thor – the giants were his enemy and he spent much of his time killing them.

Found on a farm at Akureyri in Iceland, this small bronze figure is less than 8 centimetres high and was probably made around AD1000. It represents Thor gripping his hammer.

Just as Odin was complex and crafty, Thor was straightforward and physical – the brawn to Odin's brains. Although Odin was the chief of the gods, Thor was no less revered; in fact there is some evidence to suggest that he was held in higher esteem. According to Adam of Bremen it was Thor's statue that dominated the Uppsala temple, centrally positioned between those of Odin and Freyr. Whereas Odin was favoured by nobles and kings, Thor was beloved of farmers and their families who made up the majority of the population.

That he was held in high regard is demonstrated by the wide proliferation of names with the first syllable "Thor" that are still in use. Personal names such as Thorkel, Thorir, Thorgeir and Thorbjorn were common among men, while Thorgerd, Thorbjorg, Thordis or Thora were often chosen for women. Literature also provides several examples of men having their names changed in honour of Thor. Similarly, place names beginning with the element "Thor" are distributed throughout Iceland: Thorshofn (Thor's Haven) and Thorsnes (Thor's Headland) can be found in at least five different locations. Norway has another Thorsnes, as well as Thor's Rock (Thorsberg), Thor's Island (Thorsey) and a number of places called Thor's Temple (Thorshof).

Thunder was said to be the sound of Thor's huge chariot driving across the sky, and his eyes were red, fierce and flashing, as befitted a god of thunder and lightning. His power over storms rendered his blessing vital for those making sea crossings. Although the other gods rode to their daily assembly, Thor had to walk, wading through rivers and striding over plains, because he was so

Thor Loses his Hammer

When his hammer Mjollnir – crucial to the gods' security in Valhalla – was stolen, Thor had to suffer great humiliation to retrieve it. His comical attempt at cross-dressing endangered its recovery.

When Thor discovered that his hammer was missing, he shook with fury, roused Loki, and told him the news. "Come with me" said Loki urgently, and led him to the goddess Freyja, whom they asked to share her ability to turn into a feather and travel to foreign lands. "I would give my gift for that purpose, even if it were made of gold or silver. Anything to find Mjollnir," said Freyja.

Loki flew off and found Thrym, Lord of the Giants, who asked him why he had come. "Have you hidden Thor's hammer?" Loki asked immediately. "Yes," replied Thrym. "I've hidden it eight leagues underground, and no one shall have it unless I am given Freyja as my bride."

When Loki and Thor told Freyja to prepare herself as Thrym's bride, she flew into a rage and would not hear of it. In consternation, all the gods met together to discuss the dangerous situation. If Freyja would not marry Thrym, how could they retrieve the hammer?

Heimdall came up with a solution: "Let us dress Thor in bridal clothes and send him to Thrym in place of Freyja." Thor protested hotly but Loki reminded him of Asgard's fate if he did not do so. Eventually Thor was dressed in bridal finery, with Freyja's famous necklace (see page 69) around his neck and a veil over his head. Loki volunteered to go with him dressed as his handmaiden.

Thrym was very pleased to see Freyja, and ordered a great feast to be prepared. Thor ate a whole ox, eight salmon and all the other delicacies, washed down with three horns of mead. Thrym was aghast; he had never seen a maiden consume so much. "Freyja has eaten and drunk nothing for eight whole nights, so eager was she to come to Giantland," explained Loki. On hearing that, Thrym was so pleased he went to kiss Freyja, but reeled back in fright. "Why are Freyja's eyes so red and fierce?" he gasped. Loki quickly replied, "Freyja has not slept for eight nights, so eager was she to come to Giantland."

As gullible as the other giants, Thrym was satisfied and eager to proceed with the wedding. He ordered the hammer to be brought in to hallow the couple. As soon as it was laid on the bride's lap, Thor leapt up, grabbed Mjollnir and tore off his veil. Armed once again, he crushed all the giants in the hall, choosing Thrym as his first victim.

Many tiny silver hammers such as this have been excavated across Scandinavia. They are believed to symbolize Thor's hammer and were probably worn as amulets.

colossal. Inevitably his strength was matched by an enormous appetite. He easily devoured more than a whole ox during the course of a meal, and special drinking goblets had to be kept aside for him to accommodate his mammoth thirst.

Thor owned three important material possessions. Foremost was his precious hammer, Mjollnir, a weapon that struck fear into the hearts of giants or trolls, for it could never fail or miss its mark, whether raised aloft or thrown, and would always return to the hand of its owner rather like a boomerang. Mjollnir also held the power to sanctify, and was raised for the purpose of hallowing on several different occasions. Thor had two goats, named Tanngnjost and Tanngrisnir according to Snorri, who not only drew his chariot, but could also be killed for food and resurrected by holding the hammer over their skins in blessing (see page 42).

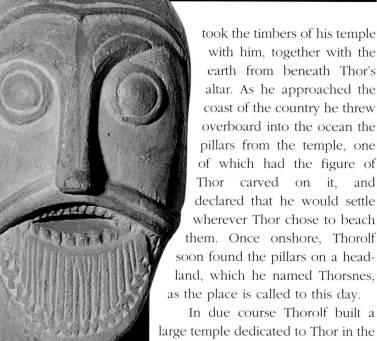

A 9th-century Viking carving depicting Thor's ominous glare. His bushy eyebrows and beard are distinctive facial features.

Secondly, Thor owned a magical belt that doubled his already formidable strength whenever he wore it. His third possession was a pair of iron gloves, without which he was unable to wield the mighty Mjollnir.

He actively sought out giants with the express intention of annihilating them; he seldom hesitated to raise his hammer in preparation for attack when he encountered them. However, there were some occasions when he saw giants as allies, or at least had some use for them: he even had two sons, Modi and Magni, by the giantess Jarnsaxa.

The most detailed account of the worship of Thor is given in *Eyrbyggja Saga*, which tells of a chieftain in Norway named Hrolf, who was a close friend of Thor and kept a temple dedicated to the god. So devoted was he that he became known as "Thorolf". When Thorolf emigrated to Iceland he took the timbers of his temple with him, together with the earth from beneath Thor's altar. As he approached the coast of the country he threw overboard into the ocean the pillars from the temple, one of which had the figure of Thor carved on it, and declared that he would settle wherever Thor chose to beach them. Once onshore, Thorolf soon found the pillars on a headland, which he named Thorsnes, as the place is called to this day.

In due course Thorolf built a large temple dedicated to Thor in the land in which he had settled. The door of the temple was in one of the side walls, and just inside it stood the high seat pillars. Beyond these the building was considered a sanctuary. In the centre of the temple was a raised platform like an altar upon which lay an armring (worn by a priest during public occasions), and a sacrificial bowl which held the blood of animals killed as offerings. People swore oaths on this altar. All the local farmers had to pay tax to the temple and support the temple priest in all his religious undertakings. The priest, in turn, was responsible for the maintenance of the temple and the organization of sacrificial feasts.

Other marks of Thor's popularity, found in Denmark and southern Sweden, are the many memorial stones dating from the ninth, tenth and eleventh centuries which bear inscriptions such as "May Thor hallow these runes" or "May Thor hallow this memorial," or sometimes just "May Thor hallow." Some stones appeal for Thor's protection merely with a carved image of his hammer. The hammer motif also appears in the shape of miniature amulets (some of them are barely two centimetres long) made of silver or base metal, which have been found placed in graves. Several have loops attached to them, which suggests that they may have been worn as pendants, and perhaps represent a pagan equivalent to the miniature cross worn by Christians.

Thor and the Giants

On one occasion, Loki mischievously persuaded Thor to visit the giant Geirrod without his hammer, belt of strength or iron gloves. The journey was long and Thor needed to take lodgings for the night. He stopped at the home of a giantess called Grid, who told Thor that Geirrod was cunning and difficult to deal with. She lent Thor another magical belt, some iron gloves and her staff, warning that he might need their protection.

As Thor approached Geirrod's court he came upon a river. Before attempting to cross it, he fastened on the borrowed belt, then waded through the water with the help of Grid's staff. But the flow of the river proved formidable and by the time that he had struggled to the middle he was almost out of his depth. At this point, he looked up and saw Gjalp, Geirrod's daughter, standing astride the river urinating to increase the torrent. Thor picked up a huge stone and threw it at the giantess to distract her. Then he made a rush for the bank and was able to grab onto a rowan tree and haul himself out to safety.

When Thor arrived at Geirrod's court, he was shown to a goatshed where he was to lodge for the night. Inside was just a single chair, which Thor sat upon, and as he did so it lifted up beneath him, pushing him almost to the ceiling. He was in danger of being crushed, but he resisted collision by lodging his staff against the roof. There was a great crack, and a chilling scream. Thor looked down and saw that the giant's two daughters were under the seat beneath him. Their backs were broken.

Geirrod then called him into the hall. As Thor entered, Geirrod picked up a lump of molten iron and flung it at him. Catching it with the help of the borrowed iron gloves, the god raised it in the air, taking aim as he did so. Geirrod ran behind a pillar to protect himself, but Thor was unperturbed: he hurled the glowing lump through the pillar, hitting Geirrod, and then continuing straight through the wall.

Not all of Thor's foes were so cunning. Sometimes, as in the story of his battle with Hrungnir, he had only to contend with brute strength. Even so, there were hidden surprises in this contest that Thor could not have anticipated.

The story began one day when Thor was away in the east, destroying trolls. Odin became involved in a horse race with the giant, Hrungnir. The two were racing so hard that the giant unexpectedly found himself inside Asgard. The Aesir

An exquisitely decorated silver cup from Fejo, Denmark (c.AD800). It would have been used by kings and their followers in carousing – a favourite activity of the gods too.

39

Thor Fights the World Serpent

Jormungand, the Midgard serpent, was Thor's adversary. The god's meeting with a giant gave him an opportunity to destroy it, which he greatly desired to do.

Thor was travelling across Midgard, having adopted the appearance of a young boy. During this journey he took lodgings at the home of a giant called Hymir who was about to undertake a fishing expedition. Seeing this as an opportunity to confront the world serpent, Thor enquired if he could accompany him. The giant looked him up and down and replied dismissively that he would not be much use as he was so small. Thor, mindful that he needed the boat, had to restrain his temper. Hymir ordered his companion to find his own bait, so Thor tore off the head of the largest ox in Hymir's herd.

They launched a boat and rowed fast, until Hymir said that they had reached his usual fishing ground. Thor insisted that they continue further, so they took up the oars again. When Hymir suggested that it would be dangerous to go any further because of Jormungand Thor ignored him and rowed on. Hymir was now very uncomfortable. Finally Thor chose a strong line with a huge hook on the end, to which he fastened the ox-head before throwing it overboard.

Deep under the sea the Midgard serpent went for the bait and swallowed the hook. He pulled away so violently that Thor was flung dramatically against the side of the boat. Summoning up all his strength, he pushed his feet through the bottom of the boat and braced them against the sea-bed. Then he pulled up the serpent. He was about to lift his hammer to strike the monster when Hymir

The giant Hymir watches Thor attack the world serpent with his hammer in this medieval manuscript

grabbed his knife and cut Thor's line so that the creature sank back into the sea. Thor threw his hammer in after it and some say that the serpent's head was struck off, but most people say that it lived on and still encircles the world.

treated him with hospitality and invited him to join them in a drink, for which they brought out the goblets that Thor usually drank from, as no others were large enough. The giant drained all of them and, as he became drunk, he began to boast, saying that he would destroy Asgard and kill the gods, all except the goddesses Freyja and Sif, whom he would carry off. After a while the gods began to feel frightened, and called for Thor. He appeared immediately and demanded to know what right a giant had to drink in Asgard. Hrungnir defended himself, saying that Odin had welcomed him personally, and it would be no credit to Thor to kill him while he was unarmed. Instead, he suggested a duel. Thor rose to the challenge at once, as he had never before been so blatantly provoked.

Hrungnir went home to retrieve his weapons, and at the appointed time and place the two met. The giants were all extremely anxious about the outcome of the duel, for Hrungnir was the strongest among them, and they felt sure that if he was killed Thor could do as he pleased.

Hrungnir had a whetstone as his weapon, and a stone shield with which he intended to avert Thor's blows. Thialfi, Thor's servant, ran to Hrungnir and told him that he was a fool to hold his shield in front of him, for Thor would attack from beneath. As giants are not very intelligent, Hrungnir naively took his advice and put the shield on the ground so that he could stand on it, holding the whetstone ready in his hands. Suddenly Thor appeared not from below but as a blaze of lightning in front of him. He hurled his hammer at Hrungnir who simultaneously threw his whetstone, with the result that the two weapons met in mid-air. The whetstone was shattered by Thor's invincible hammer which went on to smash the giant's skull.

Thor was triumphant, but in the fray a shard of whetstone had lodged in his head. Having scarcely given himself time to savour his victory, he went in search of a sorceress called Groa, the wife of Aurvandill the Bold, whom he hoped would assist him in dislodging the fragment. Groa sang spells over Thor until the piece of stone began loosen. Thor was so pleased that he wanted to offer her something in return, so he told her that her husband would be home soon; the god had

Two goats, perhaps representing his own goats Tanngnjost and Tanngrisnir, flank a "thunderstone" (a fossilized sea urchin considered sacred to Thor) in this Viking-Age brooch from Birka, Sweden. Thunderstones were believed to have dropped to earth during a storm.

waded through the river Elivagar carrying him in a basket on the return journey from Giantland. Thor said that one of Aurvandill's toes had stuck out of the basket and had frozen, so he had broken it off and thrown it into the sky where it became the star known at the time as Aurvandill's Toe (modern commentators have identified it with the morning star, Venus). However, Groa was so delighted to hear of his return that she forgot her spells, and the shard remained lodged in Thor's head.

Thor's Humiliation

The giants were helpless in the face of Thor's mighty strength, but magical art could always get the better of him. A straightforward soul, he was not wily and versed in sorcery like Odin. But even when things did not go well for him, the giants found themselves forced to retain respect for his courage in the face of adversity.

One day Thor set off in his chariot with Loki. At nightfall they arrived at a peasant's house and were given lodgings for the night. At dinnertime Thor slaughtered and skinned his goats, put them into a pot, and when they were cooked invited the peasant family to join Loki and himself for a meal. Thor placed the goatskins on the floor and gave strict instructions to the family to be sure to throw the bones onto the goatskins after they had eaten. Thialfi, the peasant's son, forgot this, and in his hunger took one of the goat's thigh bones, splitting it open to enjoy the marrow.

Before dawn Thor rose and dressed himself, raising his hammer Mjollnir to bless the goatskins. At that the goats stood up, alive again, but one of them was lame. Thor flew into a rage when he realized that the peasant's family had not obeyed his orders: the god's brow lowered, his eyes flashed and he gripped his hammer menacingly. The whole family wept, begged for mercy and offered all their possessions to the god as reparation. When he saw their fear, Thor softened and accepted their two children, Thialfi and his sister Roskva, as recompense. They became his servants and attended him diligently.

Thor left his goats with the peasants and continued on his journey with Loki, Thialfi and Roskva. Eventually they entered a huge forest, and walked through it all day, until at nightfall they came upon a building with a large entrance at one end, where they decided to sleep. In the middle of the night they were awoken by a great earthquake that shook the ground and the building. They got up and, groping around, found a smaller chamber off to the right of the main building, where Thor positioned himself, while the others, terrified, cowered behind him. At dawn Thor went outside and realized that the disturbance had been caused by an enormous giant, asleep and snoring loudly beside them. At that same moment the giant awoke and stood up; he reached so far into the sky that even Thor was afraid.

Thor asked the giant his name. "My name is Skrymir. But I have no need to enquire about you – I can see that you are Thor of the Aesir. But have you taken my glove?" As Skrymir reached down and picked up his glove Thor realized that it was where they had sheltered the night before, taking it for a building; the side chamber where they had cowered was its thumb. Skrymir asked if he could accompany Thor and his companions on their journey, and Thor, not wanting to appear cowardly, consented. The giant then suggested that it would be a good idea to pool their food, and Thor agreed, so Skrymir gathered their provisions in one bag and put it on his back.

In the evening the giant fell fast asleep and Thor took the provisions bag so that he and his companions could eat, but try as he might, he could not open it. Already tired and hungry, he was now also very angry and grasped his hammer in both hands. He brought the hammer down hard on the giant's head, but the giant simply woke up and asked whether a leaf had fallen on him.

At midnight Skrymir was snoring loudly again, and Thor approached him once more. He swung his weapon hard and it sank into Skrymir's crown. Skrymir awoke once more and said "What's happening now? Did an acorn fall on my head?" Thor backed off quickly, explaining that he had

How the Gods Gained Treasures

Dwarves were the craftsmen of Germanic mythology. Although they jealously guarded their skill and their gold, the artful Loki persuaded them to make six treasures which he gave to the gods, to the especial benefit of Thor.

The dwarves helped Loki out of trouble by forging six treasures for the gods, including Thor's hammer, Odin's ring and Freyr's shining boar.

As a mischievous prank, Loki decided to cut off all of Sif's golden hair as she lay asleep. When she awoke and discovered her loss she was distraught. When Thor heard of Loki's treachery he threatened to break every bone in his body. So, in terror, Loki promised that he would convince the dwarves to fashion a new head of hair from gold.

The dwarves agreed to help him out of trouble and please the gods. They not only made the head of hair for Sif, but also crafted the ship Skidbladnir, which, when its sail was raised, would always get a fair wind and could be fitted in a pocket when out of use. As if this was not enough, they also forged the invincible spear called Gungnir.

But Loki could not resist further scheming. He made a bet with two dwarf brothers that they could not make treasures as precious as the first three. They immediately produced three more treasures, ignoring Loki who, as a fly, tried hard to distract them.

Loki took all the treasures to Asgard. He gave the hair to Sif, and it took root on her head.

Then he gave Skidbladnir to Freyr and Gungnir to Odin, and both the gods were greatly pleased. Next, he handed over the last three treasures. The first was the gold ring Draupnir for Odin. It is said that eight rings of equal weight and value dripped from it every ninth night. Second, for Freyr, was a golden boar which ran across sky and sea faster than any horse and shed light in the darkness from its bristles. The third was a magical hammer, Mjollnir, which would never fail to strike, would never miss its target and always returned to its owner; this was given to Thor. The gods decided that the protective hammer was the best gift and stated that the dwarves had won the wager. Thus the gods owe their greatest treasures to Loki.

unexpectedly awoken and must have disturbed Skrymir, but it was only midnight and still time to be asleep. He decided that if Skrymir slept again he would strike a third blow, hard enough for Skrymir never to wake up.

Just before dawn, Thor roused himself and rushed at the sleeping giant, bringing down the hammer with all his strength. He struck Skrymir's temple, and the force of the blow was so powerful that the weapon sank deep into the giant's flesh. Skrymir simply stroked his face and said, "Are there birds in the tree above me? I am sure something fell on my face as I woke up."

Later that morning, when they were dressed and prepared to move on, Skrymir took the provisions bag and turned away from their route back into the forest. Relieved to see him go, Thor's party continued until it came to an imposing castle which dominated a flat plain. The huge gates were shut, but everyone was able to enter by squeezing

themselves between the bars. As they did so they saw a great hall, filled with giants who were seated on benches. On his throne, at the head of them all, was their king, Utgarda-Loki.

Thor's party approached Utgarda-Loki, who demanded to know what feats they could perform, "as no one can stay here with us who does not have some particular skill or talent at which he is better than other men". Loki confidently proposed an eating contest, "for no one can eat faster than I". Utgarda-Loki approved and called for a giant called Logi to compete against Loki. The two sat at either end of a vast dish filled with meat and began to eat as quickly as they could, eventually meeting in the middle. Loki had eaten all the meat off the bones, but Logi had eaten all the meat, the bones and even the dish itself. It was agreed that Loki had lost the contest.

Utgarda-Loki then turned to Thialfi and asked how he would prove himself. Thialfi was a very

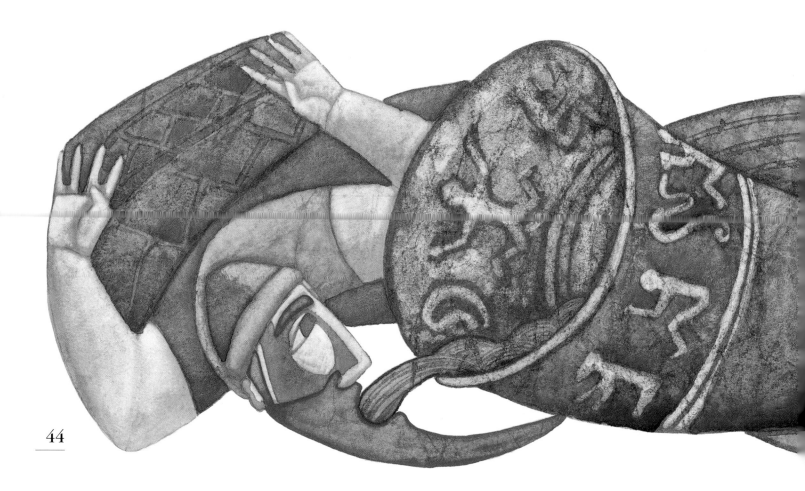

fast runner and offered to compete in a race. Utgarda-Loki asked another giant called Hugi to run against Thialfi. In the first race Hugi was so far ahead that he turned around and met Thialfi face-to-face. The second race was merely a repetition of the first. Thialfi tried for a third time, certain that he could triumph over his opponent, but when Hugi had reached the end of the track Thialfi had only run half its length. The outcome of the contest was decided.

When it came to Thor's turn, he agreed to take part in a drinking contest. Utgarda-Loki bade his manservant bring out the special horn that his men used for such events. He explained that it was considered admirable to empty the horn in one draught, although some people took two – no one was such a poor drinker that they could not drain it in three draughts. Thor looked at the horn, which did not seem very big to him, despite being rather long, and as he was very thirsty he drank in great gulps, expecting to empty the horn effortlessly. But when he ran out of breath the mead's level had hardly changed.

Utgarda-Loki said that he would never have believed anyone who told him that Thor of the Aesir could not drink more than that, but he was sure that Thor would achieve his task at a second attempt. Saying nothing, Thor put the horn to his mouth, determined to swallow a larger draught. He struggled for as long as he could hold his breath, but still he could not raise the horn as high as he would have liked. "What is the matter Thor?" asked Utgarda-Loki. "You'll be lucky to drain the horn even the third time around. Maybe you should try a different contest." Thor was infuriated, and he tried again. This time he made some impact on the level in the horn, but still failed to empty it. "Do you want to try something else?" said Utgarda-Loki, "You are obviously not going to get anywhere with this." "I will," said Thor. "What do you

The giant Utgarda-Loki challenged Thor to empty a drinking horn in no more than three draughts. Unbeknownst to Thor, the other end of the horn was dipped in the sea.

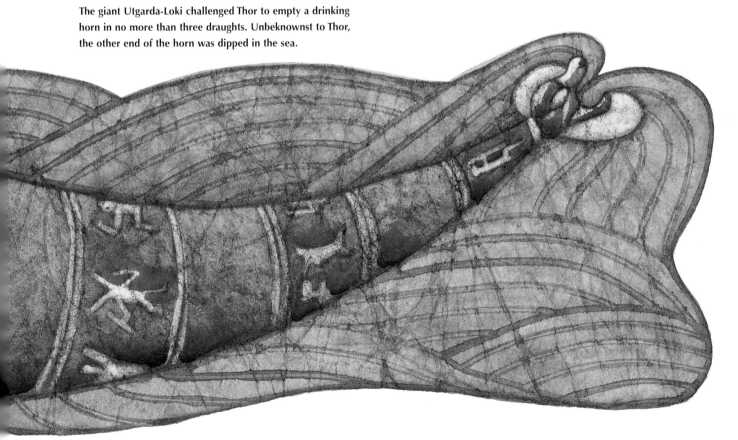

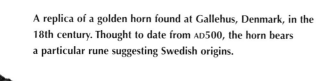

A replica of a golden horn found at Gallehus, Denmark, in the 18th century. Thought to date from AD500, the horn bears a particular rune suggesting Swedish origins.

suggest?" "This may not sound like a very great feat, but the young boys here try to lift my cat above the ground. I would not even have mentioned this to you if I had not already seen that you are a much less impressive person than I thought."

At this, a big grey cat ran into the hall and Thor grabbed it beneath the belly and tried to raise it. But the cat's back simply arched and Thor was only able to raise one paw off the ground. Utgarda-Loki watched and said, "Just as I expected. It is a big cat, and Thor is small compared to us."

Now Thor was in a violent rage and, intent on proving his courage and might, offered to fight someone. Utgarda-Loki looked around and said, "I don't see anyone here who wouldn't think it beneath themselves to fight with you, but perhaps you could take on my old nurse, Elli." Utgarda-Loki ordered the old woman to wrestle with Thor, yet the harder Thor fought the firmer she stood. Eventually Thor lost his footing and fell to one knee. Utgarda-Loki brought the fight to a halt, saying there was little point in Thor continuing with further contests against his people.

The next morning Thor and his group departed. Utgarda-Loki accompanied them some of the way, and asked Thor what he thought of his visit. Thor replied that he had suffered great humiliation. "Furthermore, I know you will say that I am a man of little consequence, which irks me."

Then Utgarda-Loki spoke: "Now that we are outside the castle I will tell the truth. While I am alive you will never set foot in my castle again: I swear that if I had known before that you had sufficient strength to bring us so close to disaster, you would never have entered in the first place.

"I tricked you with illusions: it was I that first met you in the forest. I had fastened the provisions bag with magic bonds so that you could not open it. And perhaps you noticed a flat mountain near my castle with three valleys? Those were the marks of the three blows of your hammer. I cunningly set the mountain between myself and you.

"I also deceived you in the contests. When Loki competed at eating, he rivalled Fire, which devours everything in its path. In running, Thialfi competed against Thought, whose speed no one can match. The other end of the horn from which you were drinking was dipped in the sea, so you never had a chance of draining it.

"Lifting the cat's paw was a mighty feat, for the cat was the powerful Midgard serpent which encircles the entire world. And in the wrestling you contested with Old Age, who defeats everyone, despite their strength. Now we must part, and it will be better if we do not meet again. Be warned that I will always defend my castle with similar tricks."

As Thor listened to all this he grew extremely angry and automatically reached for his hammer, but just as he was about to bring it down on Utgarda-Loki's head he found that the giant had vanished into thin air. To his astonishment, when he turned towards the castle, he found it had also disappeared. So he had to return home, very dissatisfied with his expedition.

Loki, Companion to the Gods

Loki is an ambiguous character. He was listed among the Aesir as companion to the gods, yet he was destined to become their adversary. In many of the tales, he is a typical trickster, possessed of a sense of mischief that the gods have to suffer. Yet he was also the gods' friend, often helping them out, and it was he who provided them with Thor's hammer Mjollnir, their most powerful weapon.

Loki, whose name meant "allure" or "fire", was considered to be the youngest inhabitant of Asgard even though he was not thought to be divine – in fact there is no evidence to indicate that he was worshipped at all. Paradoxically it was also thought that he existed before the beginning of the world and thus represented chaos and the unknown. But he was a cardinal figure in Asgard because he constantly subverted order, sometimes out of mischief and sometimes because of some darker intent.

In some accounts he was even described as a blood-brother to Odin – a bond that was considered sacred in the Norse community. In others he was brother to Odin and Honir, and as one of three creator-gods he gave fateful gifts to Ask and Embla, the first human beings in the world, bringing about their downfall.

A furnace stone from Shaptun, Denmark, thought to show Loki with his lips sewn up by the dwarves. This is how they punished him for refusing to yield up his head as the forfeit after they had won a wager with him (see page 43).

Loki Recaptures the Golden Apples

Ever the menace, Loki allowed his actions to threaten the gods with extinction. But it was also his resourcefulness that saved them.

Loki had the misfortune of being taken captive by a giant called Thiazi, who would not free him unless he promised to deliver to him Idunn and her precious apples of eternal youth. Always thinking of himself, Loki vowed to do this, so the giant released him.

Loki conceived a plan: he told Idunn that that she must come and see some apples in the forest which she was bound to think were precious. Once she had been lured beyond the safe confines of Asgard, Thiazi swooped down on her in the shape of an eagle and snatched her up so that he could take her to his home.

The gods were immediately affected by the loss of the youth-giving fruit and in a trice grew old and grey. Fearing for their lives, they met together to decide what to do. They discovered that Idunn had last been sighted with Loki, so they seized him and threatened him with death if he did not recover her and her apples. Loki promised to find her, and borrowed Freyja's falcon shape to fly to Thiazi's castle in Giantland. Luckily, he found Idunn there all alone, and quickly transformed her into a nut so that he could fly home to Asgard with her grasped in his claws.

When Thiazi returned and discovered his captive's escape he was furious and decided to pursue Loki: he adopted the eagle shape again and gave chase. The Aesir saw the falcon flying with a nut gripped in its claws and the eagle following closely behind. They acted quickly and built a fire in Asgard. The falcon flew over the wall and immediately dropped down to safety, but the eagle was not able to take evasive action straight away and flew directly into the flames, where it perished.

The Aesir had managed to kill the giant Thiazi, and Loki had once again wriggled out of a desperate situation.

The goddess Idunn with her magical apples was snatched up by Loki in the form of a falcon so that he could return her to Asgard. In pursuit, the giant Thiazi took the shape of an eagle.

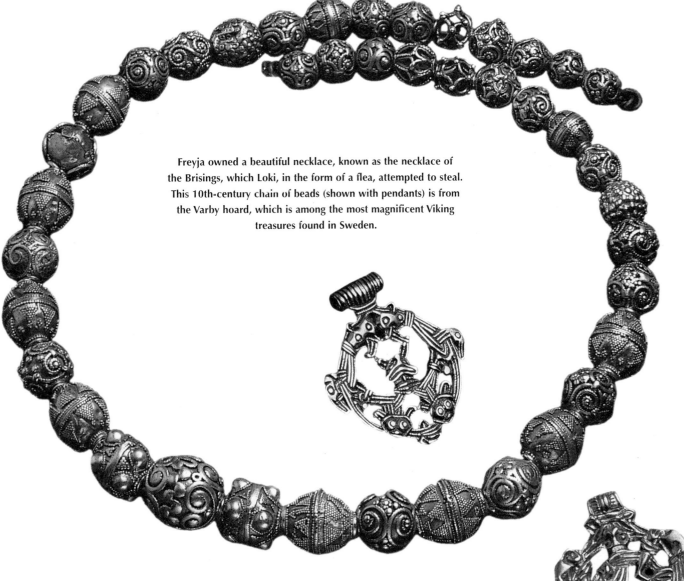

Freyja owned a beautiful necklace, known as the necklace of the Brisings, which Loki, in the form of a flea, attempted to steal. This 10th-century chain of beads (shown with pendants) is from the Varby hoard, which is among the most magnificent Viking treasures found in Sweden.

Even though people do not seem to have regarded Loki as a god to be invoked for assistance, he was the subject of many stories and played an important part in many myths.

Snorri tells us that Loki was handsome and witty, but also malicious, sly and evil. Describing him from a Christian perspective, he refers to him as the slanderer of the pantheon, the origin of all falsehood and the disgrace of everyone on earth. By nature he was restless and easily bored, which led to his gradual decline until he became a miscreant who betrayed his companions. But in most of the myths he was content living with the gods, indulging himself by playing practical jokes.

As a shape-shifter he could take the forms of animals, birds and insects. More often that not he would transform himself into an insect when he was enjoying his tricks. For example, he became a fly when he was trying to distract the dwarves from their task while they made Thor's hammer (see page 43).

Loki was not respected in the way that the other Aesir were and eventually this caused him to become bitter. His fury led to the tragic death of Balder, which set in train an irreversible series of events that would end the world.

49

Unsurprisingly Loki was descended from giants, though the circumstances of his birth were unusual. It was told that his father, Farbauti, struck stone against flint and a spark leapt into the undergrowth of a wooded island said to be Loki's mother, Laufey. Loki was thus conceived in the form of fire, which was an appropriate representation of his unpredictable nature and vast appetite.

Loki's sexual appetite was equally voracious and he mated not only with gods but with humans, animals, flora, fauna, and even with giantesses. He had three wives: the first, known as Glut ("glow"), bore him two daughters – Esia ("ember") and Einmyria ("ashes"). But Loki was not faithful to Glut, nor were Esia and Einmyria his only offspring. He had three monstrous children by the giantess Angrboda, all of whom play crucial roles in in the myths.

First was Jormungand, a ferocious, venomous serpent. Then there was Hel, a female of unspeakable hideousness. Last came the fierce wolf Fenrir, who possessed a might that seemed indom itable. They were no mere imps, but three of the most terrifying creatures in the Norse universe, and they were a significant threat to the gods. Loki also had a third wife, Sigyn, who was one of the goddesses, and they had two sons called Narfi and Vali.

The gods continued to tolerate Loki and his malign influence almost until the end of the world. They were unable to destroy his offspring, even when locked in combat. Although the three creatures posed a constant threat to the gods, fate had ordained their continuing existence.

Instead the gods had to do their best to defend themselves against Loki's mischief and his uncontrollable children. Thus Asgard was alarmed when it was discovered that Loki intended to bring the siblings to Jotunheim (giantland), as they had heard prophecies of the great harm that they would cause. The Aesir's fear of the creatures' inherent evil was confirmed by evidence of their parentage – their giantess mother was considered as heinous as their father.

Odin sent the gods to locate the children and bring them to Asgard, so that he himself could determine their fate. He decided to deal with Jormungand, the serpent, by throwing it into the sea that lay around all the lands of Midgard. There, deep in the ocean, the monster grew until, biting on its own tail, it encircled the whole world. And in this position, it brooded endlessly on how it could get its revenge on the gods.

Hel, Loki's daughter, who was described as half dead and half alive, with a grim countenance and a body that was part normal flesh and part black and livid, was thrown into Niflheim, the land of the dead, where she was to hold authority. It became her responsibility to give food and lodging to all those sent to her – mortals who died of sickness or old age rather than in battle. The monstrous wolf, Fenrir, was raised by the

Loki, companion to the gods, had all the qualities of a jester. Depicted in carvings decorating the stern of the Oseberg ship (discovered as part of a boat burial in Norway), he writhes among mythical beasts.

Aesir, although only the god Tyr was brave enough to attend to the needs of the vicious animal (see page 55).

Yet, in keeping with his ambiguous nature, Loki had other offspring who were a boon to the gods rather than a menace, and he was able not only to beget children, but to bear them as well. He was the mother of Odin's marvellous eight-legged horse Sleipnir, who was sired by the giant stallion Svadilfari (see pages 27 and 33).

Loki's maternal aspect in that myth reveals another aspect of his character – his ambiguous sexuality. Apart from giving birth to Sleipnir, it is also told in *Voluspa Hin Skamma* (The Short Prophecy of the Seeress) that he once became pregnant by eating the half-burnt heart of a woman, and from this gestation came all female monsters. *Lokasenna* relates a verbal contest between Loki and the gods in which Loki was accused of spending eight years as a woman milking cows beneath the earth, where he bore children – an activity considered most effeminate and despicable by his challenger Odin.

To insult someone using words that implied passive homosexuality was punishable in Icelandic and early Swedish law by full outlawry. It may be that the sexual uncertainties surrounding Loki described in the myths were intended to darken his character.

With the approach of the final episode of Norse mythology, Loki's character becomes less mischievous and more overtly evil. He was destined to reveal his true nature by causing the death of Balder, an action regarded by the Aesir as the most wicked ever to have happened. Even then, they were unable to punish him exactly as they wished, because he was fated to take part in the events of the final cataclysm.

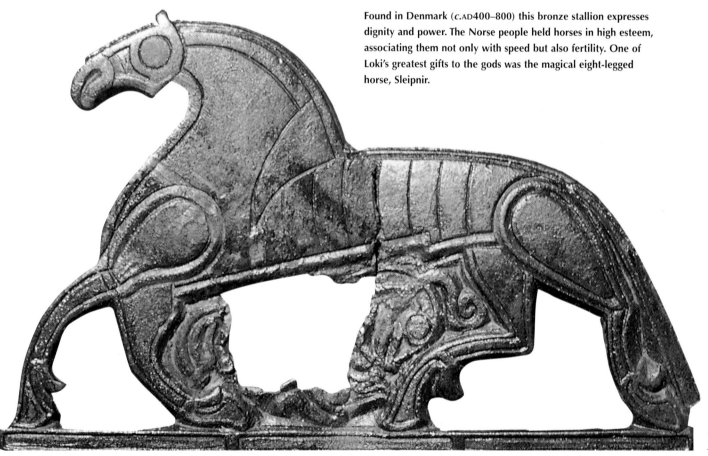

Found in Denmark (*c.*AD400–800) this bronze stallion expresses dignity and power. The Norse people held horses in high esteem, associating them not only with speed but also fertility. One of Loki's greatest gifts to the gods was the magical eight-legged horse, Sleipnir.

The Shadowy Pantheon

Asgard was inhabited by a multitude of diverse and colourful characters, but little information has survived about most of them. A large proportion of the Aesir feature only briefly in individual myths, and no further details of their connection to the Norse pantheon or of their characters survive.

The most senior member of the Aesir, after Odin and Thor, was Tyr, a war deity and the bravest and most courageous of the gods. It was held to be wise for warriors to invoke him, as he wielded great power in battle and dictated its outcome. Men who were undaunted in combat were said to be as valiant as Tyr. He was also connected with runes (the earliest Germanic alphabet), magic and wisdom, and Snorri tells that a clever man was known as "Tyr-wise". A warrior who hoped for victory was advised to carve runes onto particular parts of his sword, and repeat Tyr's name twice, which may explain why a character in the runic alphabet is called "Tyr".

Balder, the son of Odin and Frigg, is one of the better known among the Aesir, mainly due to the myths of his death (see pages 124–127). He was considered the wisest, most beautiful and most beloved of his counterparts. According to Snorri light shone from him, and an unidentified plant was once called "Balder's eyelash" because it was so white.

Balder had a wife, Nanna, who bore his son Forseti, god of justice. It was Forseti's role to settle legal disputes, and all those who came to his hall, Glitnir, in Valhalla, which had golden pillars and a silver roof, left with their difficult legal disputes

resolved. Balder also had a brother, Hermod, who features in the story of the end of the world.

The other sons of Odin remain shadowy figures. Vidar, the silent god, was said to have a strength almost equal to Thor's. He too was to feature in the battle at the end of the world (see pages 128–133), as was another of Odin's sons, Vali, whom he fathered on the giantess Rind.

Bragi (yet another son of Odin) was, like his father, a god of poetry. According to the poem, *Sigrdrifumal*, he had magical runes carved on his tongue. He was also the husband of the goddess Idunn (see page 48).

Another god who appears to have been related to Odin was Ull, the son of Sif. He was known as the ski god, the bow god or the hunting god, because his particular skills were archery and skiing. Beautiful to look at and an accomplished warrior, he was invoked by men engaged in single combat. The evidence of place names suggests that he was once a powerful deity, but sadly few stories about him have survived.

Although not a lot is known about Tyr, god of war, he appears to have been worshipped by warriors before they went into battle. A stone-carving from a 7th-century Frankish funerary monument depicts an armed warrior.

Binding the Wolf Fenrir

The gods were afraid that the huge wolf Fenrir would cause them serious harm, so they attempted to restrain him. But they could not have done it without Tyr's selfless bravery.

When the gods saw how huge Fenrir, one of Loki's malevolent offspring, was growing, they were alarmed and decided to bind him. They found a strong iron fetter, called Laeding, and suggested that the wolf pit his strength against it. Fenrir did not think much of the shackle, so he let them bind him and freed himself at once.

The gods forged another fetter twice as strong, called Dromi, and urged the wolf to try again. They said that he would become very famous if he could break free from this one. Fenrir felt even stronger now and once again broke free from Dromi with ease. The Aesir now feared that they would not be able to fully restrain Fenrir.

Odin then sent Freyr's servant Skirnir to the dwarves, and he bade them make another fetter, Gleipnir. It was smooth, soft and silky as a ribbon, but deceptively strong. The Aesir were very pleased. Fenrir looked at it carefully and said "I do not think I will gain much of a reputation by breaking such a thin ribbon, and if this band is

made by magical art then, thin as it is, it is not going around my legs." He thought again and said, "If I cannot free myself I will have to wait a very long time before you free me. But, lest you think I am a coward, I will take part in this game if one of you will dare to put his hand in my mouth."

None of the gods dared take this risk until at last Tyr volunteered to put his right hand into Fenrir's mouth. At that the wolf allowed himself to be bound, but discovered that the harder he kicked the stronger the fetter became. The Aesir all laughed – except Tyr who lost his hand to Fenrir's jaws.

The pernicious wolf, Fenrir, was brought to Asgard at the command of Odin. The gods decided to bind him with fetters to control him.

THE ART OF WARFARE

It was the right of all free men in the Viking Age to carry weapons. In the often violent times in which they lived, not only kings and nobles were involved in war; people of all ranks might find themselves called upon to fight in support of their lord, to travel with a band of raiders, or deal forcefully with a feud at home. Their favourite weapons, never far from their sides, were swords and spears – the latter sacred to Odin – and, in later times, the battle axe.

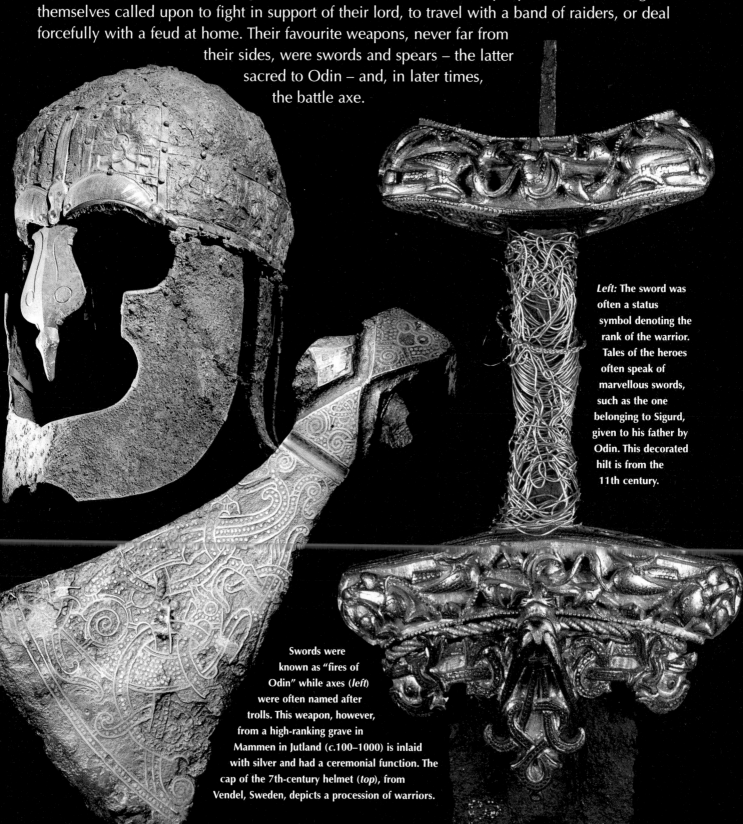

Left: The sword was often a status symbol denoting the rank of the warrior. Tales of the heroes often speak of marvellous swords, such as the one belonging to Sigurd, given to his father by Odin. This decorated hilt is from the 11th century.

Swords were known as "fires of Odin" while axes (*left*) were often named after trolls. This weapon, however, from a high-ranking grave in Mammen in Jutland (*c*.100–1000) is inlaid with silver and had a ceremonial function. The cap of the 7th-century helmet (*top*), from Vendel, Sweden, depicts a procession of warriors.

Right: This 12th-century ivory chessman was carved in Western Norway and found in the Outer Hebrides, illustrating the extent of Norwegian migration. It depicts an armed warrior mounted on a horse and wearing a helmet similar to the one shown opposite. Horses were used by the Vikings to transport their warriors, but all surviving accounts of warfare show that they dismounted once on the battlefield and fought on foot. Even Sleipnir was not used by Odin in battle.

The popular image of Vikings wearing horned helmets, such as this one from Bronze-Age Denmark, is not borne out by archaeology – no examples survive from the Viking period. However, some helmets are embossed with figures wearing crested and horned headgear. It is more than likely that these figures had symbolic significance, perhaps representing deities of war.

LORDS OF FERTILITY AND PROSPERITY

The Vanir, a group of fertility gods and goddesses, once lived happily apart from the deities of war, the Aesir. But one day this accord was shattered; different myths give different accounts of why. One relates that the Vanir, having discovered that the Aesir had welcomed the mistress of magic and evil, Gullveig, into their midst, were incensed and made lengthy preparations for war. Odin witnessed this activity with increasing anger from his high seat, and suggested that the Aesir respond by sharpening their spearheads and polishing their shields. However, the outcome of this very first war, according to one myth, was inconclusive. Eventually a truce was sealed by members of the two houses of the gods who agreed to live peacefully among each other.

In contrast to the belligerent Aesir, the gods and goddesses of the Vanir were associated with peace and prosperity: it was to them that the population prayed for healthy children, bountiful harvests and plentiful hauls of fish. These fertility deities were of great importance to the Norse people, whether controlling the land or the sea.

The most prominent of the Vanir were Njord, god of the sea, and his children, Freyr and Freyja. The names Freyr and Freyja simply mean "Lord" and "Lady". It is possible that the forms in which these two gods, along with some of the other Vanir, have survived are composites of many local fertility deities. Njord was prayed to by those seeking wealth, as well as for safety in crossing the sea and abundance in fishing. His son, Freyr, was the chief god of agricultural fertility, and regulated sunshine and rainfall, thus determining the outcome of annual harvests. Another important aspect of his role was to preside over the increase of the human population; thus he was invoked in marriage. As the goddess of love, sex and fecundity, Njord's daughter, the beautiful Freyja, is more fully characterized in mythology than the other Vanir deities. But she had other attributes, too – an expert in magic, she was able to transform herself into a bird and journey to distant lands, and she also had links with war and the dead.

Left: The couple shown here embracing have been identified as the Vanir gods Freyr and Gerd. This gold foil from Sweden was a fertility charm worn as an amulet (*c.*AD800–*c.*1000).

Opposite: Originally made in imitation of Roman medallions, gold pendants, such as this one from Sweden, were decorated with concentric circles in the Scandinavian style. This example, from the Migration Period (*c.*AD500), may have been an amulet worn for prosperity and good fortune.

57

The War between the Aesir and Vanir

The Aesir and the Vanir once lived separately from each other – the Aesir in Asgard and the Vanir in Vanaheim. Eventually, however, a bitter war broke out between them. From ambiguous accounts in the poem *Voluspa* and Snorri's *Edda* we can piece together the strange story of the conflict between the two tribes of gods and their eventual reconciliation.

The seeress who narrates the tenth century poem, *Voluspa*, declares that she remembers the very first battle in the world, fought between the Aesir and the Vanir. She tells how it started when the Aesir tried to destroy Gullveig, a woman skilled in magic (particularly in a form of witchcraft called *seid*) who had provoked their animosity by practising sorcery. They stabbed her with spears and burned her three times, but each time she rose again from the flames. Eventually, resigned to her indestructibility, they accepted her into their community.

Traditionally, Gullveig has been associated with gold and wealth. Her very name means "intoxication with gold". It has been suggested that because of her attachment to riches Gullveig was one of the Vanir, and in particular that she may have represented an aspect of Freyja who was thought to weep tears of gold, and, in her enthusiasm for precious stones, gave her daughters the names of jewels. She also acquired the glittering Necklace of the Brisings at great personal expense (see page 69).

Snorri tells two different myths about the conflict between the two tribes but does not clearly state its origins, although it is implied in his accounts that Gullveig was at the centre of the war. In one version, the gods met to discuss some disagreements between the two groups, and Odin hurled his spear into the enemy host at some point, signalling the beginning of hostilities. The war was prolonged. One side and then the other gained the upper hand, but the Aesir's stronghold was eventually shattered and the Vanir held the field. It was then agreed that members of the Vanir should live peacefully in Asgard.

In another myth Snorri describes how Odin declared war against the Vanir, and how they defended themselves and their land vigorously. Each side

Gold, jewels and riches were the province of the fertility deities. The three-pronged gold mount from Norway (above) was probably worn by a warrior, whereas the Danish gold brooch (left) was purely decorative (c.AD1000).

Guardians of the Land

Land spirits were thought to dwell in features of the landscape such as rocks, hills or rivers. They were not considered divine, but nonetheless they had the power to protect the land and its fertility.

Although land spirits were believed to bestow benign power, they also represented a malevolent force that had to be placated.

The first clause of Icelandic law, established around AD930 when the country had not yet adopted Christianity, prohibited ships with sterns adorned by dragon-heads from approaching the country. Such insignia had to be removed before the ships gained sight of the shoreline so that the spirits would not take fright and desert the land.

Belief in land spirits endured in Scandinavia long after the general conversion to Christianity. A late-thirteenth-century Norwegian law attempted to suppress the belief that land spirits lived in groves, mounds and waterfalls. Yet a fourteenth-century account reports that women continued to take food into caves or to stone piles (cairns) where they would consecrate the food to the spirits and then eat it. They did this in the belief that they would be favoured by them, and become more prosperous.

Particular features of the Norse landscape were peopled by protective spirits. This waterfall lies at the upper end of Norway's Saltdalen valley.

laid waste to the other's territory, and when at last they tired of this destruction, the two tribes met to negotiate a truce, whereby they agreed to exchange hostages.

The Vanir sent their leading members, Njord and his son Freyr, to join the Aesir. In return Honir, a handsome and accomplished figure accompanied by the wise Mimir, joined the Vanir. This part of the peace agreement proved unsuccessful: Honir was made a chieftain when he arrived at Vanaheim, but he either could not, or would not, make any firm decisions without Mimir at his side and for this reason he was considered a poor diplomat. The Vanir concluded that they had been cheated in the exchange of hostages, so they decapitated Mimir and sent his head to the Aesir. Odin embalmed the head and sang incantations over it so that he could consult it whenever he desired to gain occult knowledge.

The significance of the myth describing the war between the Aesir and the Vanir is difficult to determine, and the war itself is not described in any detail in surviving accounts. However, it appears to explain how the two types of gods, representing very different sensibilities, came to interact and coexist. It has also been suggested that the myth embodies a memory of a time when a warrior cult battled with a fertility cult for supremacy, and the two religions eventually fused. This theory is prompted by a passage in *Voluspa*, in which the established gods, the Aesir, are challenged by another race whose practices they find repellent. In the struggle for ascendancy, the Aesir eventually abandon their attempt to expel the challengers.

In stories of events following the truce, the distinctions between the gods become blurred: the warlike preoccupations of the Aesir merge to some degree with the Vanir's concerns with riches.

Njord and the Bounty of the Sea

Apart from the myth of his marriage to the giantess Skadi (see opposite), relatively little is known about Njord, father of Freyr and Freyja. He was said to be among the foremost of the Vanir and evidence suggests that he was worshipped equally among the other primary deities, but few of the stories that may have referred to him have survived.

Njord ruled the wind and held power over the ocean. Typically of the Vanir, he was primarily linked with fertility, and was called upon for success in fishing. While Thor, who also had power over the wind and waves, was invoked for sea voyages, Njord controlled the bounty of the sea, on which much of the population depended. Snorri refers to him as "Njord the wealthy" and suggests that he was so affluent he could grant lands and property to anyone who prayed to him.

Evidence deduced from place names, as well as the link between Njord and the goddess Nerthus (see page 68), suggests that in early times Njord was widely worshipped. The element "Njord" is widespread in the names of old settlements in eastern Sweden and western Norway; some of these mean "Njord's temple" or "Njord's grove", implying that they were sites of worship.

The only other evidence that we have of Njord's status in the pantheon is his inclusion in the oath pledged to the major deities by participants in judicial trials. Those invoked on such occasions were "Freyr, Njord and the almighty god" (probably Thor). Toasts were also drunk to "Freyr and Njord" to secure peace and prosperity, and in literature the names of the two gods often appear together, especially in the verses of the great tenth-century Icelandic poet, Egil Skallagrimsson. By the end of the pagan period, however, Njord appears to have been eclipsed in importance by his son Freyr.

A coastal scene in Norway. Njord was a guardian deity of the ocean and was prayed to for wealth and success in fishing. He was thought to dwell apart from the other gods in his home on the coast of Asgard.

Njord
and Skadi

The mountain goddess Skadi was the daughter of the giant Thiazi whom the Aesir killed after he had stolen the golden apples of youth (see page 48). She arrived at Asgard determined to avenge her father and punish the gods. The Aesir, hoping to placate her, offered her the pick of all the unmarried gods.

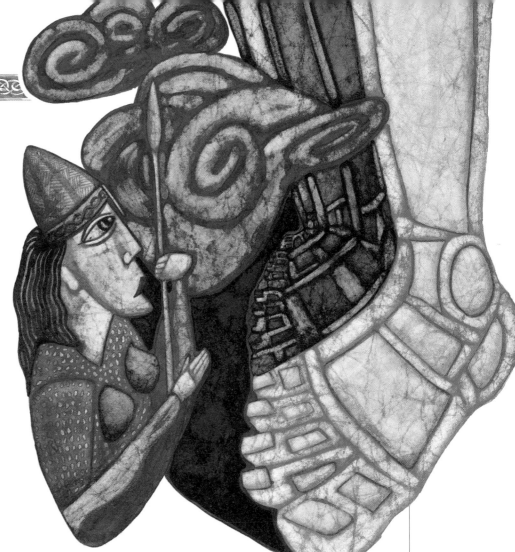

In full armour Skadi must have made an impression upon the Aesir. Repenting the death of her father, they were eager to soothe her wrath by aiding in her quest for a husband. But the gods make nothing easy for the giants or their offspring; a parade was carefully arranged in which only the gods' feet were visible.

Skadi picked the pair that was by far the cleanest, whitest and best-kept. She felt confident that they belonged to Balder, the fairest of all the gods, desired by every woman, and on this basis she claimed her husband.

Then the owner of the feet was made to reveal his identity. Instead of Balder, Skadi had chosen Njord, god of the sea, whose feet were pristine because the sea continually washed over them. At first, Skadi was taken aback, but she agreed to the marriage anyway.

The partnership was a difficult one; Skadi was the daughter of a mountain giant, and longed to live in her peak-top sanctuary, but Njord did not feel comfortable anywhere other than by the sea. Determined to fulfil their vows, they agreed to compromise by residing for nine nights in Thrymheim, Skadi's mountain castle, followed by nine nights at Noatun, Njord's coastal abode.

But this arrangement, alternating between one location and the other, failed to satisfy either Skadi or Njord – each was desperately unhappy in the other's home. Njord could not bear the dark foreboding mountains, surrounded by the eerie sound of howling wolves,

The mountain goddess Skadi was told to pick a husband from among the single gods in Asgard. But she was allowed only to see their feet in making her choice.

and Skadi could not tolerate the vast expanse of sea and complained bitterly about the screeching of the gulls.

Eventually the two were forced to live apart; Njord remained by the sea while Skadi returned to the mountains, where she was often to be seen roaming the slopes, travelling about on skis or snow-shoes.

The Mighty Ocean

The Norse people regarded the sea not only as a source of food and a means of travel, but also as providing opportunities for fame and glory. The Vikings, in particular, won prestige from their prowess in sailing and their mastery of the ocean. Just as it formed a major element in the daily lives of much of the population, so the sea was a familiar background to many of the myths, especially the ploughing of Gefjun, Thor's fishing for the World Serpent and Njord's marriage to Skadi.

A Viking ship – the greatest technological achievement of the age – under sail, albeit with a symbolic crew of only two. It has been suggested that the ship depicted in this eighth-century Gotland picture stone is carrying dead warriors to join Odin's army, the *Einherjar*, in Valhalla.

Njord was the best-known god of the sea, but another deity, Aegir, also held sway over it. While Njord was guardian of the coastline and protected and oversaw sailing and fishing grounds, Aegir personified the ocean and symbolized its mighty strength. Aegir dwelt in the depths of the sea, far from the security of land, where navigation and fishing were extremely difficult and where travel was fraught with danger. The Vikings were particularly conscious of his outstanding power; they gave the River Eider an epithet, "Aegir's Door", to lend the watercourse the grandeur of the ocean. Metaphors employing Aegir's name occur, too, in Viking poetry; for example, sinking ships are described as being swallowed by his jaws.

Aegir and his wife, Ran, held themselves apart from the Aesir and Vanir, dwelling in a golden underwater palace on the ocean floor where they were thought to receive those who drowned at sea. In some stories they are described as actually using a net to ensnare sailors. It was considered prudent to carry gold at sea so any who drowned would arrive at Ran's dwelling bearing gifts. It was also believed that the appearance of the spirits of drowned seafarers at their own funeral feasts meant that Ran had given them a particularly good welcome.

Aegir and Ran produced nine giant daughters, who each represented different types of ocean waves. They had names such as Gjalp ("Howler") and Greip ("Grasper") that were typical of giantesses. These nine daughters have been identified with the nine giant mothers of the mysterious god Heimdall, who was said to have been sired by

Odin when he copulated with all nine wave-maidens simultaneously.

Egil Skallagrimsson, in *Sonatorrek*, a famous poem which tells of his grief for his drowned son, speaks of avenging himself on Aegir, whom he held responsible for his tragic loss. Egil also refers to him as the "Ale-brewer", suggesting that the god revelled in entertaining guests. Other literary sources refer as well to largesse and the bountiful feasts held in his hall. The banquet that provides the setting for the poem *Lokasenna* was hosted by Aegir, and Thor's journey to visit the giant Hymir was instigated by the need to obtain a cauldron large enough to contain the mead to serve to the guests at another of Aegir's feasts.

Yet even Aegir's powers were dwarfed by those of the monster Jormungand, who was destined to rise out of the ocean and defeat him.

Dragon Ships

The Vikings' remarkable success in raiding and colonizing parts of Europe and beyond owed much to their navigational skills and their excellent ships. The magnificent Viking longboats were made with iron rivets attaching overlapping planks to a central keel plank which swept upwards into a stem at each end (a style known as "clinker-built"). The prows were often decorated with elaborately-carved figureheads depicting dragons or monsters, and colourful shields were hung by warriors over the sides of the vessels. The ships were propelled by oarsmen sitting beneath the top deck, fifteen or sixteen to a side, and further power was provided by a large square sail. Beautiful in appearance and easy to manage in rough waters, they were one of the great technological achievements of the Viking Age.

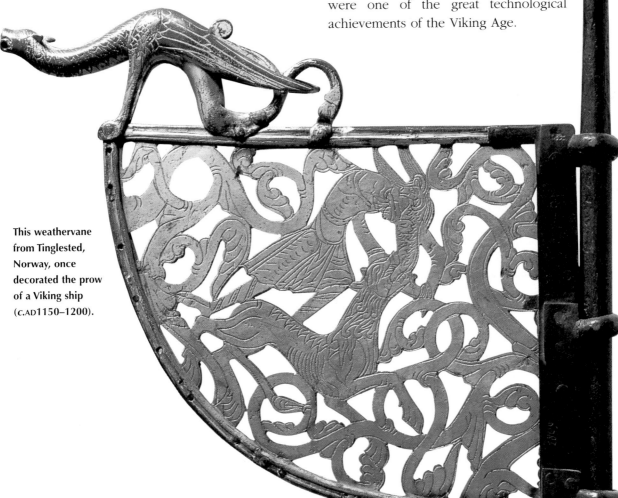

This weathervane from Tinglested, Norway, once decorated the prow of a Viking ship (*c.*AD1150–1200).

Early in the history of the Germanic peoples, ships, horses and cattle became associated with fertility rites. This impressive Bronze-Age rock carving from Bohuslan, Sweden, includes several examples of Viking boats with animal heads at their prows.

It is hardly surprising, therefore, that the ship was a powerful symbol in Viking religion. In Scandinavia, the ship appears in rock carvings from as early as the Bronze Age and appears to be linked to fertility deities: often it is portrayed alongside images of horses (also associated with fertility gods), and sometimes next to a symbol of the sun. It is known that models of ships were offered to the gods as sacrifices – in Denmark one hundred small boats of gold were found buried. They had been packed into a jar, one inside another, each with a symbol decorating its side.

Ships also played an important role in burial customs. A magnificent ship burial of a woman was discovered at Oseberg in Norway. Probably dating from the ninth century, it appears to have had some connection with the gods of the Vanir (see pages 20–21). Other ship burials found in Norway and Sweden, contained female corpses.

These were burials of rich and influential members of the community, but ordinary people were also sometimes buried either in boats or accompanied by effigies of boats. Furthermore, many graves were marked by stones laid out to form an outline of a boat beneath which the corpse or cremated ashes were interred. In various parts of Scandinavia people were also buried alongside parts of boats, recognizable after excavation from iron nails that had not decomposed. And according to Saxo, the legendary King Frodi executed a law to the effect that any chief killed in battle must be cremated in his own boat; the bodies of dead men of lesser rank were burned in groups of ten to a ship.

The Icelandic sagas mention the ship burials of two priests of Freyr. In that of Thorgrim

Viking graves were often marked by the outline of a ship such as this one from Alborg, Denmark. Although the rich and influential could be buried in exquisite wooden boats, more humble decedents might be commemorated in this way.

described in *Gisla Saga*, a huge stone was flung onto the ship before the grave was closed. This practice was also followed in the Oseberg burial.

Ships also feature in the legends of early Scandinavian god-kings, the supposed ancestors of Scandinavian royal houses. Several stories follow the same pattern in relating the journey of a young child, apparently associated with fertility, who crossed the sea in a ship and became king. One example, from the Old English poem *Beowulf* (see pages 86–7), tells how Scyld Scefing, the mythical first Danish king, came to Denmark. Accompanied by rich treasures, Scyld was put to sea at an early age. His arrival was mysterious, suggesting that he had divine origins, while his name, Scefing ("sheaf of corn"), has obvious fertility implications. Other versions of the story of the arrival by ship of a mysterious child actually place a sheaf of corn at his head.

The text of *Beowulf* also describes in detail how the Danes gave an elaborate ship funeral for the same Scyld, who departed over the sea after death just as he had arrived early in life. The poet relates how the dead king's ship was prepared for its final journey, more splendidly equipped with weapons of war, swords and mailcoats than any other vessel. The hold was stocked with valuable gifts to accompany the king on his journey. They were, the poet claims, as splendid as those treasures that came with him on his arrival as a child. The royal corpse was then laid on board by the mast, and a golden standard was set above the body, whereupon the ship was launched into the ocean and was carried away. The poet remarks that none of the grieving nation would ever know the destiny of its cargo.

Freyr, Lord of Fertility

Snorri relates that both Freyr and his sister Freyja were extremely beautiful and immensely powerful. As the radiant and bountiful god of sunshine and increase, Freyr was considered the most glorious of the gods. He is known to have been widely worshipped, although the forms of this worship have been lost.

Peace and fertility appear to have been closely linked in Norse religion: sacrifices to attain each of them were often made simultaneously, and the fertility gods had special responsibilities for keeping the human population free of strife and warfare. Accordingly, because Freyr was considered a god of peace, weapons were banned outright in his temples and bloodshed in the places that were sacred to him was taboo.

Freyr's importance is such that in the great temple at Uppsala his statue stood alongside those of Odin and Thor. Adam of Bremen was scandalized to report that the Uppsala idol had a huge phallus, symbolizing Freyr's role as god of human procreation and male potency; as for the practices attending his worship, the chronicler merely stated that they were too obscene even to describe. Saxo also commented disapprovingly on Freyr's worship; he found the gestures of the priests effeminate and unmanly, and he too declined to describe what he saw in further detail. Although Freyr's function was very close to that of his sister, Freyja – who governed sexual desire and about whom we know a great deal – we do not have much detailed knowledge of his cult, only these occasional glimpses of the rites surrounding it.

Freyr is represented in this 11th-century bronze figurine from Sweden. As a fertility deity, he was invoked at weddings where sacrifices would be made to him by those wishing the newly-married couples well.

Freyr's Treasures

Freyr owned two particular treasures. One was the ship, Skidbladnir, given to him by the dwarves, which was said always to attract a fair wind when launched (see page 43). Although it was large enough to hold all the gods fully armed, it was so skilfully constructed that it could be folded up and kept in a pouch. Freyr's other magical possession was the golden boar Gullinbursti ("golden bristles"), which could travel through the air faster than any horse could gallop, and whose brilliant metallic lustre lit up the darkest of nights (see page 43).

Freyr was particularly associated with horses, which the sagas suggest were dedicated in sacrifice to him. The horse sacrifice was particularly popular in the Migration period, which it may have first become involved in his worship. That the horse cult was important is indicated by remains of bones and hide found at sites in Sweden. Equine remains are also often found in Viking graves, particularly inside ship burials.

There are literary references to horse sacrifices too, most famously in *Hrafnkel's Saga*. Although this late work, unlike most others, does not seem to be rooted in historical fact, it can be

Freyr Falls in Love

Gerd (whose name is linked to the Viking word for "field") personified the cornfield. Held in the clutches of the giants she was unable to flourish and needed the help of a fertility god to break her wintry internment. All the same, Freyr's emissary, Skirnir ("the shining one"), who represented the sun, had to use all his wiles to persuade her to escape.

One day Freyr went into Hlidskjalf and sat in Odin's high seat, forbidden to others, from where he could see over all the universe. However, it did him no good – he went away full of woe, for he had looked to the north and seen a beautiful woman, and had fallen hopelessly in love with her.

The woman he had spotted was Gerd, the daughter of two giants who refused to let her leave their mountain home. It was said that when Gerd lifted her arms, light was shed over both the sky and the sea, and all the worlds were made bright by her beauty.

Freyr withdrew into himself and no one dared approach him. Eventually his father Njord, overcome with anxiety, sent for Freyr's servant, Skirnir, and asked him to try to discover the source of Freyr's unhappiness.

Skirnir asked Freyr why he was so downcast. Freyr confided that he had fallen in love with Gerd, "and if I do not have her as my wife I fear I will not live long. You must ask for her hand in marriage on my behalf, and bring her back here whether her father agrees or not. I shall reward you well for it." Skirnir replied that he would do this if Freyr gave him his magnificent sword, which could fight on its own. Overcome by love-longing, Freyr handed it to him straightaway.

Skirnir travelled to Gerd's home, only to discover that she was reluctant to marry Freyr. Initially, Skirnir offered her riches – the golden apples of youth and Draupnir, Odin's gold ring – which she refused.

Skirnir then threatened violence, but still Gerd refused to marry Freyr. Eventually, Skirnir warned that he would curse her with bewitchment and the gods' wrath. At this Gerd yielded and promised to come to Asgard nine nights thence.

When Skirnir returned with the news, Freyr thought he would never be able to survive that long without his beloved. He did, however, and Freyr and Gerd finally married.

Freyr fell in love with Gerd, who was so beautiful that light shone all around her when she raised her arms to the sky.

Sacred Wagons

Fertility deities seem to have often been taken on special journeys in decorated carts. In particular, the goddess Nerthus was carried around the country in a wagon with the express purpose of blessing the land and ensuring good harvests.

The Roman historian Tacitus described the rites of an early Germanic goddess, Nerthus, also called Mother Earth, who was worshipped by several tribes in Denmark. This goddess was alleged to travel among her people in a sacred wagon, which no one but her priest was allowed to touch or look into. The wagon was kept in a grove on an island during the time when the spirit of the goddess was thought to be absent. When the priest sensed that the goddess was present (it is not known how he determined this), he made arrangements for the wagon to be drawn by oxen throughout the land.

The precious time that the goddess spent among the people was a time of peace – no hostilities were permitted – and the goddess was welcomed wherever she ventured. She then returned to the sacred grove, and the wagon, with its covering cloth and contents, was ritually washed in a lake. Afterwards, the slaves who had performed this task were drowned.

The name Nerthus is cognate with that of the Old Norse god "Njord". The sexual ambivalence this implies has been explained in different ways: it has been suggested that Nerthus was a hermaphrodite deity, or that both a male and female deity formed a divine pair with a single name. Closely intertwined divine couples were not unusual among Nordic fertility deities – Njord married his sister, and Freyja was said to have co-habited with her twin brother Freyr.

An archaeological find has confirmed the ritual significance of wagons. In a peatbog in Dejbjerg, Denmark, two beautifully constructed, elaborate examples have been discovered. Similar to the one found in the Oseberg ship burial (see pages 20–21), they were probably used in ritual worship such as that described above, and interred as an offering. These wagons date from around the time that Tacitus was writing, *c.*AD100.

A detail from one of two exquisitely-carved wagons (*c.*AD100) found in a bog at Dejbjerg, Denmark.

taken to confirm Freyr's connection with horses. The saga relates how Hrafnkel, known as Freysgodi ("priest of Freyr"), loved no god more than Freyr, and shared all his most valuable possessions with him. He had a magnificent stallion of which he was particularly fond, which he called Freyfaxi ("mane of Freyr") and dedicated to the god. According to the saga, Hrafnkel vowed that he would kill anyone who rode the horse. Unfortunately when someone did so it was his own unwitting shepherd. The story details the consequences of the killing when Hrafnkel felt he had to honour his word – the vicissitudes of revenge and the inevitable battles that followed.

When Hrafnkel was finally defeated by the shepherd's family, who had become his enemies, they seized Freyfaxi and killed him by tying a bag over his head, attaching long poles to his sides and a stone to his neck, and pushing him over a cliff. This elaborate method of destruction follows a procedure that is known to have been used for killing creatures held to have supernatural powers. The cliff in Iceland where he perished, according to the saga writer, was called Freyfaxahamar ever afterwards, although its exact location has since been forgotten.

Horses dedicated to the god are mentioned elsewhere: *Vatnsdaela Saga* tells of another horse, with a similar name – Freysfaxi – whose owner had considerable faith in Freyr. A story about the Christian King Olaf Tryggvason tells how he set out to destroy the temple of Freyr at Thrandheim (the modern Trondheim) in Norway. There he came upon a stud of horses said to belong to Freyr which were kept to be killed in ritual ceremonies and offered as food to the god. Olaf showed his contempt for Freyr by mounting the only stallion in the stud while his men mounted the mares, and together they rode to the temple to destroy the god's statue.

The Swedes traced the ancestry of their kings to Freyr, and their ruling house was known as the Ynglingar after "Yngvri", an alternative name for the god in that country. According to a tale in Snorri's *Heimskringla*, the gods had once lived and

A forbidding mounted warrior is shown on this 7th-century stone from Mojbor, Sweden. For a warrior people, the horse was a valued and revered creature, even if it was not actually ridden in battle. However, among the Norse people the animal appears to have been sacred to the fertility god Freyr, rather than to the warlike Thor.

ruled on earth. When Freyr had been king of the Swedes for a time, peace, harmony and affluence came upon the land. When he passed away, news of his death was suppressed by his attendants, who secretly placed his body in a mound and paid a tribute of gold, silver and copper to him for three years in order to maintain peace and prosperity. When, after three years, the community eventually discovered the truth of his death, they were convinced that the offerings to him had kept their land free from strife, so they continued to venerate him.

The Passionate Goddess

Freyja, goddess of erotic and sensual love, was adept in the practice of magic. She played a crucial part in many of the myths and has a distinctive and well-drawn character. Stories portray her as desirable, strong-willed and passionate, and describe the consequences of the lust she inspired in others.

Freyja is the embodiment of sensuality and pleasure, and was usually portrayed in Norse mythology as the most alluring of all the goddesses. It was desire for her that motivated the giants in their assaults on fortifications around Asgard. For example, when an unknown giant builder offered to build a wall around Asgard, he demanded that Freyja be given as his wife (see pages 26–27). Then Thrym, lord of the giants, went to the trouble of stealing Thor's invaluable hammer, Mjollnir, so that he could claim Freyja in marriage as the price for its return (see page 37). And when the giant Hrungnir, drunk and over-confident in Asgard, threatened to kill the entire pantheon, he excluded Freyja and Sif, whom he intended to keep for his own delight (see pages 39–41).

Freyja was also a goddess of human love, and was invoked by men and women alike in affairs of the heart. It was said that she delighted in romantic poetry, and was considered to be the most magnanimous of the goddesses. Yet, strangely, there are few myths that centre on Freyja herself. Although she was always a significant member of the pantheon, ranking in importance beside Thor, Odin, Loki and Freyr, she mainly appears in stories about other gods.

Her husband was said to be Od, or Odur ("passionate"), who because of his name has been identified with Odin. Od was consumed by an urge to travel (a preoccupation also associated with Odin) and he spent little time with Freyja. The goddess herself travelled the land in search of him. She was said to shed tears of pure gold over his waywardness; indeed, Snorri says in his *Prose Edda* that gold can be described as "Freyja's tears". Yet despite her apparent grief at his absence, many myths allude to her promiscuity.

Freyja's sexual appetite was remarked upon by a variety of characters. The giantess Hyndla accused her of chasing after men at night like a nanny goat in heat, and when Loki insulted all the gods in the poem *Lokasenna*, he claimed that Freyja had taken every god and elf as a lover.

Freyja's desires extended beyond sexual love. Her longing to own the Necklace of the Brisings led her to have sex with four dwarves in order to secure it as her own. This was only the most famous of her many gold possessions; she had a constant lust for gold and for beautiful things, in keeping with her luxurious character. Her passionate nature could also turn to wrath; she was so infuriated by Thor when he tried to force a marriage between her and the giant Thrym (see page 37) that the halls of the gods shook with the strength of her anger, and the Necklace of the Brisings around her neck burst violently asunder.

This tiny bronze fertility figure, which stands only 6 centimetres high, is possibly an early representation of Freyja. It was found in Jutland and dates from the Middle or Late Bronze Age. The raised hand suggests that the goddess is driving a chariot.

The Lure of the Necklace

As soon as she saw it, Freyja knew she had to have the Necklace of the Brisings. The chain was made by four dwarves, renowned for their prowess in working with gold, and they were not prepared to part with it lightly.

One day Freyja chanced upon the home of four dwarves who were engaged in working gold, their usual occupation. She saw that they were fashioning an exquisite necklace, the like of which she had never seen before. As she looked at the beautiful chain she coveted it. She was certain that no neck other than hers should be adorned by such a jewel.

She offered to buy the necklace from the dwarves, but they replied that it was not for sale. Freyja offered them everything she had of value, but the dwarves were immovable.

The more stubborn the dwarves became, the more Freyja wanted the necklace; she was soon consumed by her desire to own it. Eventually the dwarves named their price: "We have all we want, there is no object you can offer us, Freyja. The only thing we truly desire is you. If you will spend one night with each of us, then we promise to give you the necklace and it shall be yours to take away."

When Freyja first saw the necklace that the dwarves had made she was overwhelmed by desire for it.

Taken aback, Freyja reflected on the dwarves' proposal. Her desire for the necklace was insuperable, and four illicit nights did not seem a high price to pay. Besides, thought Freyja, no one would know. So she agreed to the dwarves' terms.

Freyja was as true to her promise as the dwarves were to theirs; the necklace became her most prized possession.

Sacred Boars

Boars have been associated with fertility since prehistoric times. In Norse religion the boar came to be particularly sacred to Freyr and Freyja, who both owned and rode them, and could possibly transform themselves into the form of a boar. Images of boars have also been found on ceremonial objects from early Sweden and from Anglo-Saxon England.

Freyr was the owner of the marvellous golden boar Gullinbursti ("golden bristles"). Boars were also offered as sacrifice to Freyr, to ensure a good harvest. *Heidrek's Saga* describes how a boar was offered to Freyr at Yule; the largest boar that could be found was killed, and the animal was considered so holy that men laid their hands on it and swore binding oaths. Those who consumed the flesh of the sacrificial boar felt that they were ingesting the god himself, and assimilating his power.

Freyr's sister, Freyja, had the nickname Syr ("sow"), and was possibly visualized in this form. Freyja also rode a boar, called Hildisvin ("battle swine"). The poem *Hyndluljod* tells how Freyja disguised her human lover, Ottar, as Hildisvin to enable him to gain information from the wise giantess, Hyndla. She rode him alongside Hyndla while she questioned her and Ottar listened.

Swedish kings were also said to treasure helmets decorated with images of boars. A boar-crested helmet mentioned in the poem *Beowulf* apparently protected the life of the wearer.

This bronze boar, c.400BC, is only 6 centimetres long.

Although Odin's gracious wife, Frigg, was the queen of the gods, it was Freyja who captured the hearts and minds of the Norse people. In fact the two figures have even been identified as aspects of one goddess; according to this theory Frigg represented the dutiful, nurturing wife and mother, while her obverse, Freyja, was the passionate mistress and lover. The two goddesses shared certain roles: they were both invoked during childbirth to protect and assist women in labour (the elder tree, which was sacred to Freyja, was thought to help alleviate the pain of childbirth) and the two were involved in the naming ceremony of newborn children. Furthermore, they were both known for weeping. While Freyja grieved for Od, Frigg mourned for her dead son Balder (see page 126).

Freyja, Shamanism and Seid

Freyja possessed another powerful aspect that gave her predominance among the Norse deities – she was believed to be endowed with the ability to transform herself into a falcon or the shape of a feather (a power also attributed on one occasion to Frigg), which enabled her to fly like a bird to other lands. Only Odin shared this shape-shifting ability, a fact that underlines Freyja's status among the gods. The power to change shape or to take leave of the physical self and be transported elsewhere is associated with shamanism, a form of spiritual practice particularly common in Arctic and Central Asian religions, but also known in many other parts of the world. The shaman can journey in spirit to other worlds, and can go into trances to obtain information either from the gods or from the dead on behalf of his community.

Odin displays certain features of shamanism. For example, his self-sacrifice on the World Tree that won him the magic runes (see pages 30–31) is reminiscent of Siberian initiation rites in which the young man or woman training to be a shaman has to undergo a ritual death and rebirth, experiencing torment and suffering in order to acquire spiritual knowledge and powers.

Among the Norse deities it was Freyja, however, who was especially adept in the type of sorcery which in the Viking world was most similar to shamanism. *Seid*, as this was known, could be used in pre-Christian Scandinavia for divination, and although a man might conduct the rites, it was usually a woman, known as a *volva* or seeress, who did so. The seeress carried a staff, and is described in one account as wearing a special costume made from the skins of animals and from feathers of various birds, all of which represented spirits from the animal world who assisted her on her spiritual journey. During the ceremony the seeress sat on a high platform, and incantations were sung to summon spirits who would reveal occult knowledge to her. This enabled her to enter into a trance, during which she would descend to the netherworld.

Seeresses of this type travelled the land, visiting farms and attending feasts to perform their rites on behalf of the people. They were often consulted on the destinies of individuals, the prospects for potential marriages or the abundance of the harvest. If a community was plagued by famine, *seid* might be employed to divine its outcome. Because *seid* was usually practised for the benefit of the community, *volvas* were welcomed and honoured wherever they went.

The best-known account of a seeress's visit is given in the saga of Eric the Red. The visit is said to have taken place in an Icelandic settlement in Greenland, and the ceremony is described in fascinating detail: the *volva* wore a costume fashioned from animal skins, which included a hood made of black lambskin lined with white cat's fur, calfskin boots and fur-lined gloves made from the hide of cats. She carried a brass staff, and wore a necklace of glass beads around her neck.

The ritual began with the presentation of a sacrificial meal, prepared from the hearts of every

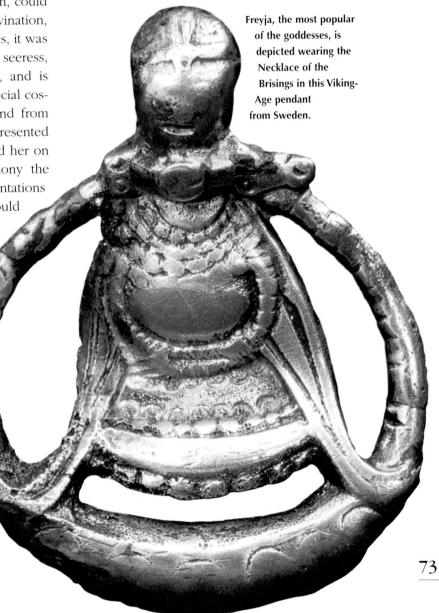

Freyja, the most popular of the goddesses, is depicted wearing the Necklace of the Brisings in this Viking-Age pendant from Sweden.

73

Human and agricultural fertility are clearly linked in the imagery on this Bronze-Age cremation urn from Denmark. Not only were both concerns of Freyja's, but these were the two issues that seeresses were most frequently consulted about.

Frejya introduced *seid* to the Aesir. She was also associated with cats, who were said to draw her chariot on journeys, and whose importance in *seid* is implied by the use of their fur in the *volva's* costume. *Seid* was at the core of communal fertility rites, and provided the answer to questions about love, marriage or harvests – all areas superintended by Freyja as a fertility deity. The travels of the *volva* around the country also resembled the journeys of sacred wagons to communities around the land.

A *volva* is mentioned in a mythological context in the series of events leading up to Ragnarok, when Odin travels for nine days from Asgard to Niflheim, the land of the dead, to find answers to his questions about the fate of the pantheon (see page 124). The figure whose counsel he considers worth such a long and hazardous journey is a dead sorceress. The poem about the destruction and creation of the world, *Voluspa*, is also narrated by a seeress whose wisdom is unquestioned.

However, there was a darker aspect to *seid*. According to the sagas, its power could be utilized malevolently to cause serious harm to particular enemies or even to kill them; sickness, misfortune and insanity could all be summoned by the practitioner of *seid*.

Heimskringla tells us that it was thought shameful for men to practise *seid*; usually only priestesses were taught the necessary spells, although the *Laxdaela Saga* has an account of a young boy killed by male sorcerers employed by his father's enemies, who directed *seid* at him. It is possible that these men practised a form of sorcery appropriate to their sex; however, in an act clearly motivated by repugnance at a perversion, King Harald Fairhair set fire to his own son's house and burned him alive, together with eighty of his followers, because they had all participated in *seid*.

living creature that could be found, given to her as she sat on a high platform on a cushion stuffed with hens' feathers. A young girl chanted a spell, for which the *volva* praised her afterwards, telling her that her singing was so delightful that many spirits had come to listen, allowing her to gather a great deal of knowledge from them. Having awoken from her trance and answered the girl's questions about her own future and fortunes in marriage, the *volva* turned her attention to the crowd, replying to any queries put to her by individuals about their prospects. The saga claims that little she foretold went unfulfilled.

Goddesses and the Fates of Men

Many minor goddesses graced the Norse pantheon, and almost all of them were fertility deities. Some had personalities of their own, while others appear to have been merely aspects of major goddesses such as Freyja and Frigg. A number of the figures celebrated as goddesses were giantesses who had gained divine status by marrying into the pantheon.

In the *Prose Edda* Snorri names many goddesses, some of whom are barely mentioned elsewhere. One of these is Saga, whom he ranks just below Frigg. Other sources, however, suggest that she may have been merely an aspect of Frigg: she appears only once in the *Poetic Edda* in a passage that tells of her home Sokkvabekk ("sinking beck"), a place washed by cool water, similar to Frigg's home, Fensalir ("house of the fens"). There, Odin and Saga are described spending their days happily drinking from golden cups, but it is more likely that it would have been Frigg, Odin's wife, who would have spent such leisurely days with her husband. Furthermore, Saga's name means "seeress", and Frigg was the deity of divination.

Hlin, who was said to watch over those whom Frigg wished to protect, also appears to be another appellation for Frigg herself. She is mentioned in the poem *Voluspa*, which describes her sorrow in anticipation of the time when her husband, Odin, must face the wolf Fenrir in combat at Ragnarok. The literature mentions three other little-known goddesses who personify qualities belonging to Frigg: Vor, who was so wise that nothing was hidden from her, and the sage and

Norse goddesses were associated with black magic by Christian critics. This wood engraving (dated AD1555) from the workshop of Olaus Magnus, entitled "Concerning the Magic Women", depicts Scandinavian witchlike figures causing a shipwreck.

Skadi, the mountain goddess, was associated with winter and the harsher aspects of the Norse climate. Her unsuccessful marriage to the sea god Njord may stand for the meeting of winter and springtime fertililty, and their mutual irreconcilability.

courteous Snotra ("Wisdom") and Syn ("Denial") who watched over the doors of the gods' halls in Asgard, denying access to those who were not permitted entry. Other goddesses are described as Frigg's attendants. For example, Fulla and Gna, her handmaidens, had the tasks of carrying her casket, attending to her shoes and sharing her secrets.

While Frigg was the goddess with whom the minor deities shared most attributes, some had similarities instead with Freyja. Sjofn was much occupied in turning both men's and women's thoughts to love, while Lofn was kind and benevolent: it was to her that the people addressed prayers concerning marriage. She was thought sometimes to obtain Odin and Frigg's approval of a union even if the course of love had not hitherto run smoothly. Var listened to matrimonial oaths and private promises between lovers and meted out punishment to those who broke their vows.

There were also similarities between the goddess Gefjun and Freyja: one of Freyja's names was Gefn, and both goddesses received women after death. Both were associated with fertility – Gefjun's famous act of ploughing (see opposite) linked her with agriculture, and the names "Gefn"

and "Gefjun" both derive from the verb meaning "to give". In spite of looking after dead virgins, Gefjun, like Freyja, had an extremely healthy sexual appetite, and Loki accused her of wantonly trading sexual favours for a necklace just as Freyja had done (see page 71).

Some fertility goddesses were giantesses who gained divine status by virtue of their marriages to gods. Like Gerd (see page 67), Skadi, Freyr's wife, came originally from a race of giants. After her marriage to Njord Skadi was accepted into the ranks of the Aesir, despite their living apart. She is often mentioned alongside the other goddesses, and appears to have been worshipped in her own right: in *Lokasenna* she is made to list her holy groves and shrines. Up in the mountains on her skis and snowshoes, Skadi was clearly a goddess of winter, and the myth of her marriage to Njord, a god of fertility (see page 61), appears to serve a similar meaning to that of Gerd's marriage to Freyr: the ending of the long harsh winters and the arrival of spring. The changing of the seasons was of real concern to the people of northern Europe, though in the myth of Skadi the emphasis is on the incompatibility of the seasons.

The Ploughing of Gefjun

The origin of the island of Zealand, upon which Copenhagen now stands, is explained in a myth about the goddess Gefjun. It is told that she was responsible for separating this land from mainland Sweden by tricking the Swedish king with cunning and magic.

The goddess Gefjun spent some time with King Gylfi of Sweden, giving him great pleasure. Unaware that she was a member of the Aesir, he offered her as a reward as much land as she could plough with four oxen in one day and night.

Gefjun then coupled with a giant and bore four sons to him.

She transformed her children into oxen and harnessed them to a plough. With this mighty team she ploughed the ground so hard that she detached a whole district which the oxen pulled the land far out into the Baltic Sea. There Gefjun established it as an island and gave it the name of Zealand.

A huge lake – now called Lake Malar – remained in Sweden where the land had been uprooted. It has been remarked that the inlets in that lake match the peninsulas on Zealand.

Gefjun gave birth to four sons, sired by a giant, whom she transformed into a team of oxen.

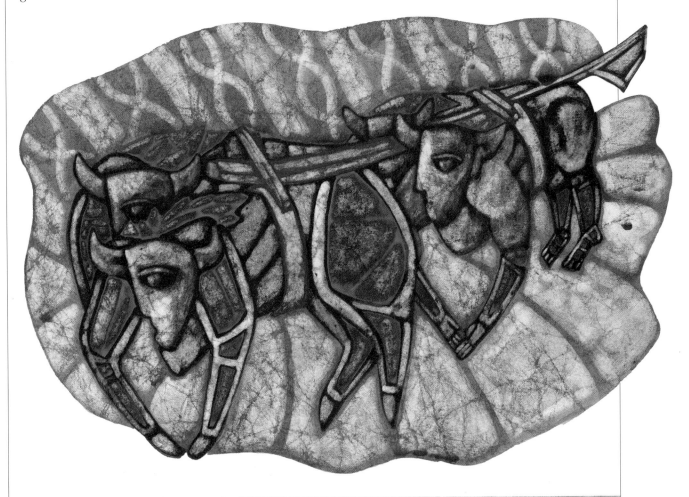

TRIUMPH OF THE HERO

Writing for Roman readers, Tacitus praised the German ethical code: how chieftains and their followers strove to outdo one another in courage, how warriors would be ashamed to leave the battlefield alive if their leader had fallen, how young men travelled abroad in search of war, how warrior chiefs rewarded their retainers with gifts, and exchanged gifts among themselves, and how men took up the feuds of their kindred. All these motifs recur in the legends, from the early lays and epics such as those about Bjarki and Beowulf, to late compilations like the Dietrich cycle.

Most early Germanic and Scandinavian tales which have survived the centuries are concerned with human heroes, not gods and goddesses. They may seem to modern readers to be sensational and bloodthirsty adventure stories, but in their own time they were far more than that: they offered role models for aristocrats and warrior elites, and a morality based upon honour, courage, loyalty and revenge. The hero's task was to fight, either for his own honour or in the service of his king, and to endure death with unflinching courage; his reward would be fame and wealth in his lifetime, and (even more importantly) a glorious and enduring reputation after death. As the Icelandic poem "Havamal" (in the *Poetic Edda*) puts it: "Kinsmen die, riches depart, every man must die himself; I know one thing that never dies – the fame of a dead man."

Below: A 14th-century book illustration shows a tournament victor receiving a wreath. Many Germanic legends have survived in 13th- and 14th-century retellings reflecting chivalric ideals.

Christianity tolerated these violent and vengeful tales, although the many explicit allusions to heathenism originally contained in them were discarded or played down. As we know from a letter from Alcuin to the Bishop of Lindisfarne in AD797, true heroic legends were thought unsuitable entertainment for monks, who, the great churchman complained, ought to listen at mealtimes to sermons rather than lays about heathen kings. On the other hand, Saint Olaf, King of Norway, had the ancient Lay of Bjarki sung to hearten his army before battle, and long after England became Christian the kings of Wessex had scenes from the Volsung legend carved on the walls of their banqueting hall in Winchester. So long as the security of a kingdom depended on the loyalty and discipline of its fighting men, heroic ideals still had value in society, and stories enshrining them were likely to survive.

Opposite: A 19th-century painting of Germany's Black Forest. Mysterious natural sites have been associated with Germanic legends.

Legends and Themes

In Germanic and Scandinavian legends, heroes were not demigods or supernatural beings. They may have possessed magical qualities, such as the ability to change shape, but essentially they were merely men gifted with courage and endurance. The stories' impact depended on the values embodied within them, often expressed through timeless situations – the will to avenge a slain kinsman or a confrontation with a superior and terrifying force. The legends of these heroes can still stir our hearts and win our admiration.

Some Germanic tales relate to historical figures (such as Ermanrich, Attila the Hun, Gunther, Theodoric and Alboin), who lived during the fourth to the sixth centuries, and the legends about them may have begun circulating soon after their deaths. But many heroes (Bjarki, Sigurd or Siegfried, Grettir and Beowulf) seem to be fictional, even though all their stories are set against historical backgrounds.

Moreover, historical facts are often distorted in the legends. The Huns, for instance, were not Germanic at all, but Mongolian nomads who conquered some Germanic territory, yet their leader, Etzel (the real-life Attila), was treated just like any Germanic hero, without mention of race.

The hero is not an isolated individual, but is firmly bonded into society by a network of mutual obligations – ties of kinship and allegiance – in which one man is bound to defend another to the utmost. These bonds are supreme and unbreakable; tragedy arises if one conflicts with another.

The carved wooden doorway of Hylestad church in Norway depicts scenes from the legend of Sigurd (c.AD1100). Here Regin, the blacksmith, is reconstructing Sigmund's sword.

Personal pride and honour also imposed obligations which could result in tragedy. Friendship could be as strong a tie as kinship, especially if formalized by oath; for example, part of the tragedy of the story of Sigurd was that he swore such an oath with Gunnar, the Burgundian, (who was also his brother-in-law), then betrayed him afterwards and orchestrated his murder. There was a third powerful bond – the one between a king and his followers, especially the select few who made up his bodyguard.

In most of the older tales, the hero's crowning achievement is his death – the taste for happy endings came later. Just as Germanic gods were ultimately doomed to be destroyed in battle, so for the individual hero luck would eventually change, the protection of Odin would be withdrawn and death was inevitable. It was essential to meet death with defiance – thus both Gunnar the Burgundian and Ragnar Lodbrok allegedly died without fear, one playing the harp, the other laughing.

Walter and Hagen

For Germanic heroes, death was no tragedy; far more distressing was the dilemma when a man found himself trapped between conflicting loyalties, as in the tale of Hagen and Walter.

Etzel (Attila) the Hun had taken three hostages: Walter of Aquitaine and Hagen the Frank (who had both sworn friendship to each other), and Hildegund, who was to be married to Walter. However, all three escaped, taking Etzel's gold with them.

They reached the Rhine, in Hagen's homeland, and news of their coming was brought to Gunther the Frankish king, who felt he had the right to take the gold from them by force as Etzel had plundered his lands. Hagen, as Gunther's vassal, was bound by oath to assist him and so left the other two.

Walter and Hildegund encamped in a pass among rocks and there Walter prepared to fight. Gunther sent twelve Frankish warriors against Walter, and one by one they were slain, including a young nephew of Hagen. Tragically torn between honouring two sacred bonds, Hagen himself would not fight his friend, though Gunther taunted him with cowardice. He and the king withdrew.

At dawn, Walter and Hildegund left their cave, only to be ambushed in open country by Gunther and Hagen. This time, Hagen joined in the attack, to avenge his nephew. Fierce was the fight of two against one, ceasing only when all three were maimed. Then at last the warriors made peace.

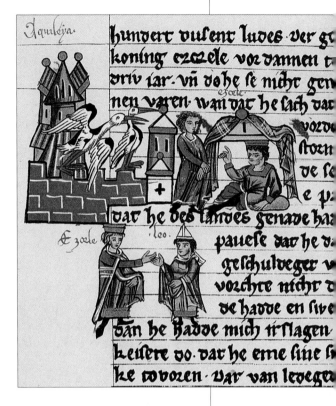

Attila the Hun sits on a throne in a 13th-century manuscript illumination. The legend of Walter and Hagen begins with their capture by him.

In the Middle Ages European literary fashions became apparent in German poetry. The chivalric codes of Arthurian romances saw piety, courtly grace and delicate emotions added to the old virtues of loyalty and courage to create new ideal heroes such as Lancelot and Parzifal. Resolution and happy endings were preferred: old material was revized to suit these tastes. One of the major medieval accounts of the old Germanic legends, the *Nibelungenlied*, is still essentially a tragedy based on a lust for gold and vengeance, as the Volsung legend was; but it is also full of tournaments, elegant clothes and picturesque feasts, as in chivalric romances. The sorrows and conflicts of its characters are more openly expressed than the terse style of older poetry allowed. The scale is broader, too; its final battle scenes involve a background of thousands of anonymous slain knights.

Other German tales bring in characteristic medieval themes; it is love rivalry, not revenge, that drives the plot. In the legend of the minstrel Tannhäuser, the ancient theme of a hero drawn into the Otherworld becomes a Christian story about sexual temptation, sin and salvation, and the goddess who welcomes him is no longer called Freyja, Holla, or a Valkyrie, but Venus.

Gradually the powerful concepts of Germanic heroism merged into general European culture, to be rediscovered in their full force by scholars and creative writers many centuries later.

81

Bothvar Bjarki, the Battle Bear

At dawn on July 29 1030, as King Olaf Haraldsson of Norway prepared for battle, he asked his court poet to sing, loudly enough for the whole army to hear. The poet gave them a very old song, the *Lay of Bjarki*. It was one of the best loved of the heroic lays, expressing the themes of the warriors' code: unflinching courage, loyalty, the longing for glory, joy in battle and defiance in the face of death.

according to some sources, their enemies used magic and called up the dead to fight on their behalf. All the champions except one died on the battlefield; the survivor avenged his lord by offering to swear loyalty to the victor, seizing the sword on which the oath was to be sworn, and killing him before dying himself. "And so," says one chronicler of the man's short-lived triumph, "he was the only man who has ruled the Danish kingdom for barely six hours."

Bjarki's part in this last great battle was a strange one. Hrolf's warriors had been asleep when the enemy attacked at dawn, and whereas all the others awoke, seized their weapons and rushed out, Bjarki remained behind, apparently still sleeping. Again and again his friend Hjalti tried to rouse him, urging him to remember his duty. Now was the time for warriors to awake, said Hjalti – not for slumber – now was the time for them to keep their oaths to defend their king and repay him with their blood for all the fine weapons and gold that he had given them. By such courage, they would become famous in every land, and fulfil the boasts made when drinking. Brave men must face their enemies, like eagles grappling with their prey.

The original lay sung by the poet that day is lost, apart from a few lines, but Saxo and other later writers report that Bjarki was the greatest among twelve champions who formed the bodyguard of King Hrolf Kraki of Denmark – a historical ruler probably living around AD550, whose real life became obscured by a rich embellishment of legend. Like Arthur or Charlemagne, Hrolf was served by warriors whose fame equalled his own. He and his champions were remembered for their heroic deaths in a battle where they were taken by surprise and heavily outnumbered, and where,

This 13th-century manuscript illustration shows combatants, richly clothed in knightly regalia, engaged in a tournament. Such combats were popular events in which knights displayed their heroic qualities for entertainment.

Still Bjarki did not answer or move, though by now King Hrolf's hall was ablaze, and Hjalti taunted him, asking why he chose to be burned to death when he could find a nobler end in battle. Then at last Bjarki replied: "Let us go and die with our king. I shall lie by his head, and you by his feet, and eagles and crows will eat us. In death, dauntless men should lie around their king." Hrolf duly fell, and all his bodyguard died with him.

But why was Bjarki so slow to act? The lay does not explain, for such poems were composed for audiences who already knew the basic story and did not need to have it spelled out for them. However, the full story can be found in the Icelandic *Hrolf's Saga* of about AD1400 (although its source is probably as old as the lay itself): the secret lies in the hero's name, which means "Little Bear", and in the ancient belief in shape-changing, the strange, innate, magical power by which some people could either turn physically into an animal, or send out their spirits in animal form while their bodies lay in a trance.

Hrolf's Saga tells how at the beginning of the battle a huge bear was seen at the head of King Hrolf's men, always very near the king. He slew more men with his paw than any five of the king's champions; blows and missiles glanced aside from him, and he trampled men and horses underfoot, crunching his victims between his teeth.

In the *Lay of Bjarki* it is the human body of this champion that was slumped and motionless indoors. When Hjalti finally managed to rouse him, he sighed deeply, and said to him "You have not done the king such good service as you think. The battle would almost have been over by now, but Fate must have its way, and no plan will help us. I tell you, I can give our king far less help now than I was giving him before you called me." And when the two of them went back to the field, the great bear had vanished and the tide of battle had begun to turn against King Hrolf's men.

The Icelandic story also explains where the hero gained his bearlike nature by drawing on a widespread folktale about a man who was a bear's son. It explains that Bjarki's father was named Bjorn ("Bear"), and his mother Bera ("She-Bear"); Bjorn had actually been transformed into a bear by his stepmother, a witch. In this source the hero is called Bothvar Bjarki ("Battle-Bjarki"). He was immensely strong, fearless and generous to those weaker than himself, including Hjalti, a runt who had been the butt of Hrolf's warriors until Bjarki befriended him and gave him courage by making him drink the fortifying blood of a monster.

In the Germanic world, a hero's worth was measured by the manner of his death, and all other details of his achievements took second place. Despite their other achievements, it was the last stand of Bjarki and King Hrolf's other champions which won them their fame.

Bears were admired for their strength and courage, so a bearlike nature was appropriate to a great warrior. This scene illustrated a 13th-century German manuscript.

The Death of Beowulf

Although composed in England in the eighth century AD for a courtly and Christian audience, the story of Beowulf is set in sixth century AD pagan Scandinavia. Beowulf himself is a legendary figure whose name means "Bee-destroyer" (or "Bear"), implying that he may originally have been thought of as a shape-changer.

For several generations after first arriving in Britain, the Anglo-Saxons remained aware of their Continental ancestry, and legends of Germanic heroes were retold in English poetry.

The story of Beowulf opens at Heorot, the royal hall of the Danes, which the aged King Hrothgar had been powerless to defend against a man-eating ogre, Grendel. Young Beowulf, living in the land of the Geats, southern Sweden, heard of this, and sailed to Denmark to offer his services to the king. Using his great strength and cunning Beowulf destroyed Grendel, only to confront the creature's mother, incensed with grief.

He wrestled with her in her underwater lair, a magical place where breathing was possible. Beowulf would have died had he not found a sword there, better than his own, with which he beheaded her.

As a result, Beowulf became king of the Geats, and reigned in peace for fifty years. But then trouble shattered the kingdom's serenity. A dragon which had long guarded a treasure hoard was robbed of a golden cup, and flew over the countryside, burning everything in its fury. Intending to face the monster alone but accompanied by warriors, Beowulf set out for the ancient burial mound where the creature hid. Striding towards the tumulus, he shouted aloud, challenging his foe. The dragon glided out, and the fight began. Beowulf's sword pierced the scaly skin, but struck a bone, and glanced aside; deadly flames flared around him. Terrified, the watching champions fled to the woods – but one, brave young Wiglaf, ran to the aid of his lord. The serpent turned its fire against him too. Wiglaf sheltered behind Beowulf's iron buckler, and together the two men attacked their foe. Beowulf drove his sword deep into the dragon's skull just as the monster sank its teeth into his neck. But Wiglaf plunged his sword into its belly; the fires died down, and, though mortally wounded, Beowulf ended its life by ripping it open with a knife.

Soon, the warriors who had hidden in the woods returned. Wiglaf reproached them: "You and your kinsmen will be stripped of all you own and driven away; everyone will know how you fled. You would be better dead than to live in such shame!"

Then the Geats built a pyre, heaping weapons and treasures upon it. Woodsmoke rose, black above the blaze, as Beowulf's body burned. Finally, they sang his praises as the most gentle of men always eager for fame.

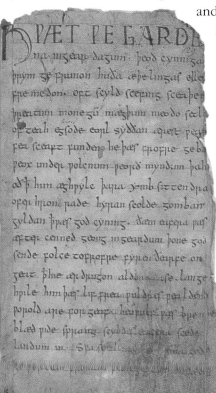

A fragment of the original manuscript of *Beowulf*, the 8th-century English epic based on a 6th-century Scandinavian story.

Dragon-Slaying

Just as in real life men have always tested their courage and strength in hunting as well as in warfare, so in myth and legend gods and heroes proved themselves in combat with fierce or monstrous beasts – bears, lions, serpents, and, above all, dragons.

Germanic dragons were visualized as huge, often terrifying serpents; they breathed fire or poison, swallowed their prey, or killed them by coiling around them, like a boa. Sometimes, but by no means always, they had wings and legs. To drink their blood or bathe in it gave strength, wisdom or invulnerability.

They had a great love of gold, and the hero's motive in attacking them was often to win treasure as well as glory; saving a king's daughter, which was a frequent element in romances and fairy tales, was a much rarer event in the older heroic texts.

Sometimes the dragon-slayer was a young man, and such an exploit was his first step on the path to glory, as was the case with the Volsung heroes (see pages 88–91). But elsewhere a dragon-fight was a warrior's last and greatest battle, in which both he and the monster perish; in myth, this was Thor's fate, while in epic it was Beowulf's.

Germanic tradition, unlike the Bible, does not present dragons as morally evil, but simply as fierce and dangerous creatures.

Dragons were common creatures in medieval tales not only in Germany and Scandinavia, but across Europe, as shown in this 14th-century French manuscript illumination.

Fafnir, the dragon whom Sigurd slew, was ancient and deeply wise, and was able to foresee the future. The poet who wrote *Beowulf* spared a few words of pity for the dragon as he met his death: "The air had once been his delight, his nocturnal realm; now he was death's prisoner, and had enjoyed his earthy cavern for the last time."

Tannhäuser, the Minstrel

In reality, Tannhäuser was a poet famous for his passionate love songs who served at the court of Frederick the Belligerent, Duke of Austria, from AD1230 to 1246. After Frederick was killed in battle, Tannhäuser fell into poverty and was forced to live the uncertain life of a wandering minstrel; what became of him nobody knew. But this very mystery gave rise to the legend by which he is still remembered today.

In the prime of his life, Tannhäuser, the noble knight and poet, came by chance upon a mountain which was reputed to be the entrance to the Underworld. It may have been either Blocksberg or Mount Hörsel in Thuringia, where pious folk believed they had seen uncanny fires and heard the pitiful shrieks and moans of sinners' souls. All agreed that women of the Otherworld lived there; learned men said they must have been led by the goddess Venus of whom Ovid and Virgil had written, but whom peasants spoke more readily of as kindly Mother Holla.

Tannhäuser decided to see for himself what truth there was in the rumours, and rode boldly to the foot of the mountain. At once a door opened for him in the rockface, and beautiful women came to meet him, inviting him to join their dance and feasting. He accepted with amazement and delight, and they led him to their queen, whose beauty surpassed anything he had thought possible, for she was indeed the Lady Venus herself.

Tannhäuser remained inside the mountain for what he thought was only a few days. In great joy and contentment, he wrote songs in praise of Venus and her ladies, and enjoyed all the pleasures that they could offer. But then, remembering his knightly duties, he decided it was time for him to return to the world, and asked Venus to show him the way out of her realm.

Shown in this 14th-century German manuscript, Tannhäuser was a historical figure of the 13th century. His disappearance is explained in legend as the consequence of being tempted to join Venus in her mountain den.

She, however, was most unwilling to lose him. She told him he could stay for ever, and have whichever of the ladies he liked best as his wife and companion; moreover, she said, he had in reality been inside the mountain for a whole year, and his friends probably all thought him dead. At this Tannhäuser angrily replied that he had in fact been duped by the women and their wiles, and now wished only to return to the human woman whom he loved with all his heart. "I will not burn in Hell for all eternity for the sake of the red lips of your ladies," said he. "Let me go my ways. If I remain here my soul will sicken and die."

Venus then offered her own fair body to him, and used all her cunning to lure him to her chamber. But Tannhäuser cursed her in a loud voice, and called on the Virgin Mary to help him to escape. His prayer was heard; the mountain opened for him, and he left its luxurious magic for the harsh light of day. So great was his remorse and shame that he dared not face his lord or his beloved; instead, he travelled alone and on foot to Rome, and begged Pope Urban in person to hear his confession and impose some penance upon him so that his soul might yet be saved.

Witches, as depicted in this medieval woodcut entitled "The Journey to Blocksberg", were believed to embody licentiousness. In the teachings of the medieval Church, Venus, Tannhäuser's temptress, was said to have dwelt in the Harz Mountains.

"Speak, son," said the Pope. Weeping bitterly, Tannhäuser knelt before him and told how he had spent a whole year inside the magic mountain, neglecting all thoughts of religion and knightly duty, and making love to the damsels of Lady Venus. Pope Urban heard him with silent horror. He gave no absolution and imposed no penance, for he thought the sin so heinous that nothing could atone for it. Instead, he broke off a dry twig from a dead shrub in the courtyard, and said, "Your sins will be forgiven when, and only when, green leaves begin to sprout from this dead twig in my hand." And he threw the twig on the ground in front of the knight.

Tannhäuser replied: "If I had only one year left to live, I would spend that whole year in repentance, hoping to attain God's mercy." "For such as you there is no mercy," said the Pope. Then, filled with misery and despair because God's earthly spokesman had rejected him, Tannhäuser left the Holy City and set off northwards once more. Now he no longer went on foot as a humble penitent, but dressed himself again in knightly finery, riding a war-horse and carrying a golden lute in his hand. And as he rode, he sang love songs to Venus and all her fair damsels.

When he came again to the foot of the mountain he cried out: "Open for me! Heaven rejects me, and if this be Hell, then Hell is what I choose for all eternity." At that, the door in the mountain opened, and Lady Venus stood there, welcoming him back as the dearest of her many lovers.

But in Rome, it was the turn of Pope Urban to grieve, for on the third day after Tannhäuser had left the Holy City, the Pope's eyes happened to alight upon the twig that he had thrown aside, and he saw freshly sprouting green leaves covering the bark. The Pope repented of his haste and arrogance, and sent messengers to all lands to find Tannhäuser and assure him of forgiveness. But it was too late, for he had already returned to the magic mountain, where all his love was given to the women of the Otherworld. And there he will stay until Judgement Day, when perhaps he will be forgiven and saved.

The Volsung Heroes

Of all Germanic heroes, the Volsung family were the most famous, celebrated in poetry, art and prose among Anglo-Saxons, Germans and Scandinavians; their tragedy is still familiar today through a cycle of operas by Wagner.

Volsung, King of the Huns, was a mighty hero, under the protection of Odin. He had many children; first came twins, a boy and a girl called Sigmund and Signy, then nine other sons. As a young woman, Signy was betrothed to King Siggeir of Gautland, and at their wedding feast an old, one-eyed man in a hooded cloak strode into the hall and drove a sword deep into the tree-trunk which supported the roof, saying: "Whoever can remove this sword shall have it as my gift, the best blade he could ever have."

All tried to pull out the sword, but only Sigmund succeeded. Siggeir offered him three times the sword's weight in gold for it, but Sigmund answered scornfully: "You too could have possessed it, if Fate had allowed; it is mine now, and you will never have it." From that moment, King Siggeir hated his brother-in-law.

Three months later, Siggeir invited all the Volsungs to Gautland, secretly planning to ambush them. Signy warned her father, but he would not flee; he was slain, and all ten of his sons were captured. At Signy's request they were set in stocks in the forest rather than being killed. Every night for eight nights a she-wolf killed and ate one of them, until only Sigmund was left. Then Signy contrived a plan to save her twin brother: she smeared his face with honey, which the wolf greedily licked.

Sigmund caught the wolf's tongue between his teeth, and in her struggles to get free she broke his stocks. Sigmund killed her, and hid in the forest.

For ten years Signy helped him to hide. Meanwhile her two sons by Siggeir were growing up and she sent them secretly to Sigmund so that he could test their courage. However, they failed, and Signy said: "Take the boys and kill them. They need live no longer." Then, seeing that no son of Siggeir's would ever be man enough to avenge the dead Volsungs, Signy approached a witch, who agreed to exchange shapes with her so that she could sleep with her own twin brother unbeknown to him.

In due course, Signy bore a son called Sinfjotli who was the epitome of a Volsung. When he was aged nearly ten, she sent him to Sigmund, who tested his courage as he had his half-brothers. Sinfjotli did not fail; in fact he astonished Sigmund by his eagerness to kill his supposed "father" Siggeir in order to avenge the Volsungs.

Together Sigmund and Sinfjotli managed to gain entry to Siggeir's halls and hid in a storeroom.

Only Signy knew that they were there. Now Signy and Siggeir had had two more sons, who were still young, and one of them happened to see the two fierce men in full armour. He ran back to the main hall, crying: "Danger, father!" At this Signy seized both children and dragged them hastily back to Sigmund and Sinfjotli. "My children have betrayed you. Kill them!" she said. Sigmund refused, but Sinfjotli did not hesitate.

Then a great fight erupted, but the odds were so unequal that despite their courage Sigmund and Sinfjotli were captured.

This ornate dragon-head was found among furniture in the Oseberg ship burial (see pages 20–21).

But Signy secretly released them in the dead of night whereupon they returned to Siggeir's hall and set it ablaze. Siggeir awoke among smoke and flames, and called out to know who had set the fire. "It was I," said Sigmund, "with Sinfjotli, my sister's son, and we want you to know that not all the Volsungs are dead."

Sigmund entreated Signy to leave her husband in the burning building, saying she could live on in high honour as his sister. But she replied, "Learn now how faithfully I remembered our father's death at Siggeir's hands: when his sons seemed unlikely to avenge the Volsungs on my behalf, I had them killed. I am no longer fit to live. Willingly I shall die with King Siggeir, unwilling as I was to marry him." Then she kissed her brother and son, and walked back into the flames.

Sigurd, Son of Sigmund

Sigmund returned to his father's kingdom, where he had many adventures and died face-to-face with Odin in battle, after his superb sword shattered against the god's spearshaft. But his pregnant wife Hjordis kept the pieces, knowing that the son she would bear would be the greatest of the Volsungs and wield the weapon once again.

Sigmund's son became the hero whom Norsemen call Sigurd, and Germans call Siegfried. Like his forefathers, he was a favourite of Odin. His own father dead, Sigurd was fostered by Regin, a clever blacksmith, who pieced together Sigmund's broken sword. Sigurd's first adventure came about when Regin urged him to seek glory and wealth by using the sword to execute the dragon Fafnir, who was Regin's own murderous, gold-loving brother, transformed.

Sigurd dug a trench across the dragon's path, and thus was able to pierce the beast from below. Dying, Fafnir warned Sigurd that the gold he had been guarding would bring death to all who owned it, but Sigurd replied that every

man must die, and that the brave desire wealth. Then Regin (who had been hiding in terror) came to drink Fafnir's blood, and asked Sigurd to roast the heart for him. Sigurd happened to touch the juices of the heart as it cooked, licked his finger, and at once found he could understand the birds in the trees nearby. They told him that the blacksmith meant to kill him and steal Fafnir's hoard. Sigurd ruthlessly cut off Regin's head, ate the dragon's heart and took the gold for himself.

Sigurd then found a Valkyrie asleep on a mountain top, surrounded by fire. He wakened her; they made love, and swore to marry one another – for she had vowed to marry only the bravest of heroes, one who could defy the flames. Sigurd gave her a ring from the dragon's hoard and left. The woman, who was named Brynhild, had conceived and was pregnant.

However, Sigurd proved faithless to his beloved. Travelling further in search of adventures, he came to Burgundy, where there was a king with three sons, Gunnar, Hogni and Guttorm, and one daughter, Gudrun. Their mother, Grimhild, was expert in magic. Seeing that her daughter was in love with Sigurd but that he loved Brynhild, Grimhild brewed a magic drink of forgetfulness for him. Thus, he was married to Gudrun, and swore friendship with Gunnar and Hogni.

Regin, who fostered the fatherless Sigurd, was an accomplished blacksmith who was able to reconstruct Siegfried's sword for his posthumous son. This Anglo-Saxon manuscript illumination from the 11th century shows a smith's assistants preparing a fire.

Peace was not to come to the family. Gunnar too discovered Brynhild and fell in love with her but could not penetrate the circle of flames, so, knowing of Sigurd's courage, he asked his friend to exchange shapes with him. Sigurd (as Gunnar) took Brynhild as his wife, although he kept a sword between them as they lay together, so that she should be untouched when the real Gunnar claimed her. As a token, he took a ring from her and gave it to Gudrun. It was the one he had given her himself before he was duped by Grimhild.

Now, Gudrun knew everything that Sigurd had forgotten. One day, quarrelling with Brynhild, Gudrun mocked her for having belonged to two men, and marrying the lesser. She showed the ring in proof, and explained how Brynhild had been tricked. Furious and humiliated, Brynhild sought revenge. She taunted Gunnar with cowardice, then told Sigurd the truth, reviving his memory. Appalled at his own treachery, he offered to carry her away, but she refused. Finally, she falsely told Gunnar that she had been possessed by Sigurd when he had wooed her on Gunnar's behalf.

Desiring revenge, Gunnar and Hogni persuaded their brother Guttorm to kill Sigurd, since, unlike them, he had never sworn friendship with him. Guttorm stabbed Sigurd as he lay sleeping, but Sigurd woke with the pain and hurled his sword at Guttorm as he left, cutting him in two at the waist. Then Sigurd died, protesting with his last breath that he had never betrayed Gunnar's trust.

At his death Gudrun wept bitterly, but Brynhild laughed and said to her husband Gunnar: "You and all your kin will suffer an evil fate because you broke your oath of friendship to Sigurd". She foretold how he and Hogni would die, and Gudrun suffer future sorrows. "And now," she said, "build a pyre for Sigurd and myself. Kill his horse, as well as four of my menservants and eleven of my waiting women. Burn them with us so that our funeral will be worthy of us both." She stabbed herself, and was burnt with Sigurd.

The gold that Sigurd had won from the dragon Fafnir passed to Gunnar and Hogni, only to bring their doom. Sigurd's daughter by Gudrun died a cruel death. But Aslaug, the daughter he had fathered with Brynhild and the last of the Volsung race, survived and, according to one legend, married a great warrior, Ragnar Lodbrok.

Heroic Cunning

Heroes often needed cleverness as much as courage. A story about Ragnar Lodbrok, who may have been the real "Ragnar" responsible for sacking Paris in AD845, shows the importance of resourcefulness.

An earl's daughter named Thora was dearly loved by her father and each day he gave her a present. One day, he sent her a pretty little snake as a pet, which pleased her so much that she put it in a box and and allowed it to sleep on her gold rings. Soon it started growing, and the gold beneath it grew too. Thora's snake became so large that it had to coil around the house and nobody was able to enter or leave the building.

Ragnar decided to win both the gold and Thora. He made breeches and a cape from shaggy fleeces. According to one version, he boiled them in pitch and rolled them in sand, but Saxo says he plunged into water on a freezing day, so that he was coated in ice. Either way, his unusual covering protected him admirably; the venom which the serpent spat at him could not penetrate it, nor could the gush of deadly blood which spurted over him as he speared the monster. Thus Ragnar killed the dragon at little risk to himself, and won Thora and her treasure.

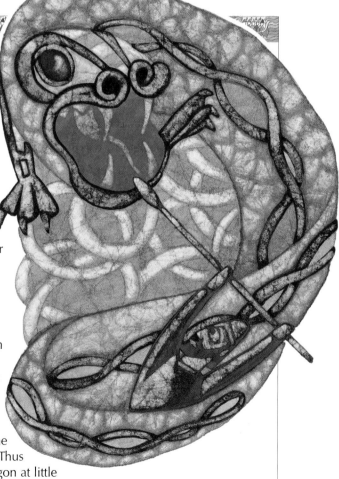

Ragnar Lodbrok spears a gigantic serpent and eludes its deadly venom.

The Gold of the Nibelungs

In AD436 the Rhineland kingdom of the Burgundians was destroyed by the Roman general Aetius, leading an army of Hunnish mercenaries. The Burgundian King Gundaharius died in the battle, together with his brothers and 20,000 men. This disaster was explained in legend as a family tragedy, peopled by characters from the Volsung legend.

The medieval German *Nibelungenlied* tells how three Burgundian brothers, Gunther, Gernot and young Giselher, ruled at Worms on the Rhine; their sister Kriemhild (known as Grimhild in the Volsung legend) was famous for her beauty and virtue. Their chief warrior was named Hagen (see page 81). At Xanten in the Netherlands lived Siegfried (or Sigurd), a peerless knight, who had already won a vast treasure in a battle against the giants called the Nibelungs, together with a magic cloak of invisibility. He had also slain a dragon and become invulnerable by bathing in its blood.

Kriemhild (Grimhild) is depicted greeting Brynhild and Gunther after their arrival at Worms in an illustration from the "Hundeshagen" manuscript of the Volsung legend. This manuscript dates from the 15th century.

Hearing of Kriemhild's beauty, Siegfried set off for Worms, won her heart, and they were married.

Now Kriemhild's brother Gunther wished to marry Brynhild, who would only take a man who could outdo her in athletic contests. Wooers who failed were slain. Because of his magic powers Siegfried accompanied Gunther to Brynhild's land, pretending to be his vassal; making himself invisible, he helped him perform the necessary feats.

So proud Brynhild was finally wed, but in the marriage chamber she drove Gunther away from her. Gunther told Siegfried; next night Siegfried came invisibly and wrestled her into submission, so that Gunther could possess her. Siegfried also took Brynhild's ring and girdle, which he gave to Kriemhild. He then gave her the Nibelung gold as a wedding gift and took her home to his kingdom.

After some years, Brynhild began to complain that Siegfried gave neither homage nor tribute to King Gunther, as a vassal should. When Siegfried and Kriemhild next visited the Burgundian court, the two queens began to quarrel. Kriemhild boasted of her husband's valour, while Brynhild retorted that he was a mere vassal.

"If so," cried Kriemhild angrily, "your rank is still lower than mine. I am his wife, you are just his mistress! Siegfried took your virginity, so how dared you marry Gunther?" Then she produced Brynhild's girdle and ring as proof.

Furious, Brynhild persuaded the warrior Hagen to avenge this insult. He enlisted Gunther to join him in a plot to murder Siegfried for his gold. Cunningly, he asked Kriemhild whether Siegfried was completely invulnerable, and she told him of a spot between the shoulder-blades that could be pierced, because a falling leaf had

Gunnar and Hogni

The Norse tale of what happened after Sigurd's death has several differences from the Nibelung legend. In this version, Sigurd's widow Gudrun mourned, but took no vengeance; she was married against her will to King Atli (Attila) the Hun, a cruel and cunning man whose sole purpose was to discover Sigurd's gold, hidden by Gunnar and Hogni.

Atli invited Gunnar and Hogni to a banquet, but Gudrun, suspecting treachery, sent them a ring carved with runes to warn them to keep away. Yet Gunnar replied defiantly, "Bring us ale in golden goblets, for this may be our final drink!"

They travelled to Atli's fortress, where armed men overwhelmed and captured them. They were imprisoned apart, and Gunnar was asked if he would buy his life with his treasure. "First bring me Hogni's heart," he said. Atli's men tried to trick him by showing him a slave's heart, but he replied scornfully that a heart which shook on the dish could not be the fearless Hogni's. So they cut out Hogni's heart while he laughed aloud and brought it to Gunnar, who cried out, "Now you will never find Sigurd's hoard, Atli! Only I know where it lies. Let the Rhine keep it, rather than Huns enjoy it!" "Put him in a wagon and take him to the snake-pit," ordered Atli. He watched while Gunnar sat chained among the poisonous creatures, playing his harp, until he died.

When Atli returned, Gudrun, having devised a plan, greeted him warmly, telling him, "I have had two young deer slaughtered to feast you." But when Atli and his men were half drunk, she jeered at him: "The meat you have eaten and shared with your men was the hearts of our two sons. You will never see them playing again."

Wild with grief, Atli drank deeper than ever. In bed that night Gudrun drove a sword

Gunnar fearlessly met his end in a deadly snake-pit, as depicted in the Hylestad church, Norway, c.1200.

through him and burnt the hall down, killing all who had helped cause her brothers' deaths. No woman since has done such fearsome deeds to avenge her kin.

shielded it from the dragon's blood. "Sew a mark on his clothes," said Hagen, "so I can protect him."

Next, Gunther and Hagen invited Siegfried to hunt and feast in the forest, and as they drank from a stream Hagen speared Siegfried in the back, just where his loving wife had stitched the sign on his tunic. Kriemhild mourned bitterly, but remained at Worms with her brothers, though for four years she would not speak to Gunther. At length they seemed to be reconciled, but Gunther wronged her once again: at Hagen's instigation, he seized the Nibelung treasure, her wedding gift. Hagen then sank it in the Rhine so only four men knew its hiding-place: Gunther, his two brothers, and Hagen himself. All swore to secrecy. Yet, proud of their new wealth, they now called themselves the "Nibelungs".

Kriemhild again appeared to forgive her brothers, but this was a sham. Hoping to avenge Siegfried's death and the loss of her treasure, Kriemhild married King Etzel (Attila) of the Huns thirteen years after the murder of her husband, and invited her kin to a midsummer feast.

The Nibelung lords, with several thousand knights, set off for Hungary, where they were joined by Margrave Rudeger with 500 men and the noble Dietrich of Bern (based on the historical figure of Theodoric the Great, King of the Ostrogoths). Dietrich warned them that Kriemhild meant them harm. But they rode on to Etzel's court, where Kriemhild welcomed Gunther with false friendliness, although she spoke harshly to Hagen. Next day a tournament was held, which ended in bloodshed when a Burgundian slew a Hunnish knight. Full-scale battle was averted

Kriemhild was forced to marry Etzel (Attila) the Hun against her will. This 13th-century manuscript of the *Nibelungenlied* shows her being presented to him.

because Etzel judged that the deadly thrust had been accidental. Kriemhild then begged Dietrich and his bold liegeman, old Hildibrand, to kill Hagen, but both considered this dishonourable.

Kriemhild therefore found another champion, who, in his quest Hagen, slew a group of Burgundians. When the news reached Hagen in the banqueting hall, he drew his sword at once and cut off the head of King Attila's son, sending it spinning into his mother Kriemhild's lap. Furious battle broke out, until Dietrich shouted, suggesting that those who were neutral agree to a truce. Then fighting was renewed, and did not come to an end until every Hun inside the hall lay either dead or mortally wounded. The 7,000 dead Huns were thrown out into the courtyard by the Nibelungs.

Further Hun soldiers besieged them. All day long they fought, and still the Nibelungs held the hall. At nightfall the two sides parleyed, but since each one thought themselves more wronged, peace was impossible. Then Kriemhild, loving her two younger brothers and holding them guiltless of Siegfried's death, offered them safe conduct if they would hand over Hagen. Indignant, they refused, so Kriemhild ordered the attackers to set fire to the hall.

As the flames rose, many complained of thirst. "Drink blood," said Hagen, "a sweeter drink than any wine." So they sucked blood from the wounded, and their strength was renewed. At dawn 600 Burgundians were still alive.

Rudeger would gladly have negotiated for peace, but Etzel was now as bitter as the queen, and urged him to fight, as a vassal should. This horrified Rudeger, but Etzel and Kriemhild pressed him until he consented. He and Gunther's brother Gernot met in the battle, and each slew the other.

Then the followers of Dietrich of Bern came forward, asking leave to take away Rudeger's body for burial. This was refused them. Enraged, the champions from Bern, save Dietrich himself, hurled themselves on the Nibelungs. Hero fought hero, until only Hagen and Gunther of the Nibelungs and Dietrich's man, old Hildibrand, were still alive.

At last, Dietrich armed himself, and called on Hagen and Gunther to surrender, but Hagen only jeered and brandished Siegfried's sword, taken from the Nibelung hoard. Dietrich wounded him, and then, unwilling to kill a weary warrior, took him captive. He did the same to Gunther, and Kriemhild had them both imprisoned, separately.

Kriemhild came to Hagen in his dungeon. "Give me the Nibelung hoard you stole from me," she demanded. "Never, while my overlord King Gunther lives," said Hagen. Then Kriemhild ordered Gunther's head to be struck off and shown to Hagen. "Now none save God and I knows where the hoard lies and you will never see it, she-devil!" "At least I have Siegfried's sword," she retorted, snatching it to behead him.

King Etzel grieved for the death of Hagen, a great warrior, though an enemy. But Hildibrand preferred revenge to forgiveness – he violently slew Kriemhild there and then.

After such carnage, the Burgundian court could not be saved and was entirely destroyed.

Jousting could be fierce and dangerous, as in this German manuscript. In the *Niebelungenlied* it led to outright warfare.

VIKING AND CHRISTIAN ART

The Christian faith, to which Scandinavian countries were gradually converted around the second half of the tenth century, did not cause a total break with tradition in the visual arts – any more than it did in poetry and tales – since craftsmen's skills could be adapted to suit new patrons. Sometimes, in the period of transition, pagan and Christian symbols appear on the same object, and it is not always clear whether they are in harmony or opposition. Often such artefacts celebrate a respect both for the ascendant religion and a continuing attachment to the waning pagan mythology that still inhabited the hearts and minds of the Norse people.

Above left: The golden orb of the Holy Roman Empire, decorated with precious jewels, originates from 12th-century Germany. Christians adapted the ball, a symbol of the cosmos and the harmonious universe, by setting a cross above it to represent a world dominated by Christianity.

Above: A silver pendant found in Iceland, only five centimetres in length, represents Thor's hammer, crucial to the protection of Asgard. The monster forming the loop is probably the Midgard serpent. The maker or owner has cut a Christian cross into the middle of the ornament.

Right: This wooden stave church at Vangsnes, Norway, is 12th century. These tall, dark churches are quite unlike most European architecture, and may replicate heathen temples. The interiors are lavishly carved, and the multiple roofs have fierce dragon-heads decorating the gable-ends.

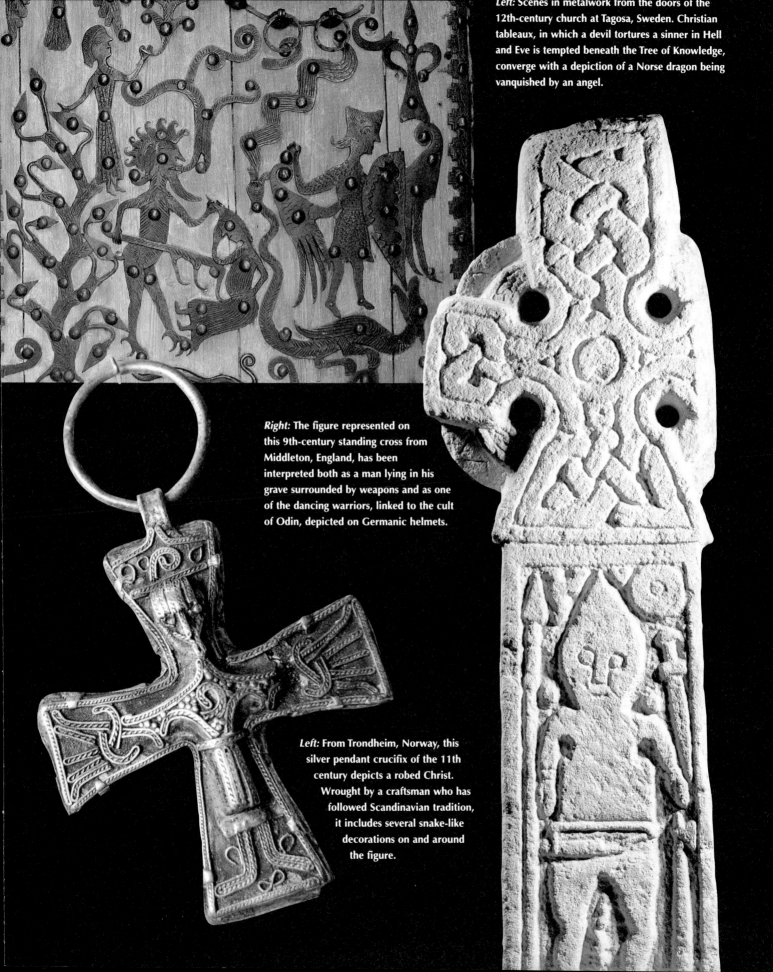

Left: Scenes in metalwork from the doors of the 12th-century church at Tagosa, Sweden. Christian tableaux, in which a devil tortures a sinner in Hell and Eve is tempted beneath the Tree of Knowledge, converge with a depiction of a Norse dragon being vanquished by an angel.

Right: The figure represented on this 9th-century standing cross from Middleton, England, has been interpreted both as a man lying in his grave surrounded by weapons and as one of the dancing warriors, linked to the cult of Odin, depicted on Germanic helmets.

Left: From Trondheim, Norway, this silver pendant crucifix of the 11th century depicts a robed Christ. Wrought by a craftsman who has followed Scandinavian tradition, it includes several snake-like decorations on and around the figure.

Gudrun of the Hegelings

By the twelfth century AD, some Germanic tales were blending ancient heroism with medieval ideals of chivalry, so that love could be the prime motivation for a plot, as in the story of Princess Gudrun and her suitors.

Hetel, one of the Hegeling dynasty, ruled the Netherlands. His son Ortwin was famous for his courage, and his daughter Gudrun for her beauty. Many wooed her, among them a Moorish prince named Siegfried, and Hartmut, Prince of Normandy, but she rejected both. A third wooer was the bold knight Herwig. He too was initially refused but he won Gudrun's heart, and King

A page from the earliest manuscript of the *Prose Edda* narrating the story of Gudrun, who was enslaved for five years by Prince Hartmut and his tyrannical mother, Queen Gerlint (*c.*1280).

Hetel agreed to their marriage the next year. Enraged at being rejected, Siegfried ravaged Herwig's lands, so Hetel and Ortwin set sail to help their future kinsman.

Now Hartmut of Normandy had spies at Hetel's court, and when he learned that the king was absent, he seized the opportunity to go and ask again for Gudrun's hand. She refused, saying she loved Herwig and was pledged to him. Then Hartmut had Gudrun captured and taken away, together with her female attendants.

When the sad news reached Hetel and Herwig they made peace with Siegfried so that all three could join in rescuing Gudrun. They caught up with Hartmut and all day battle raged, until the golden sands on which they fought ran red with blood. Towards evening, King Hetel was slain by Ludwig, the Norman king and Hartmut's father. Then, under cover of the dark, the Normans sailed away. The Hegelings and their allies had to return home, mourning the loss of their dead and their kidnapped princess.

Meanwhile King Ludwig and his wife Gerlint did all they could to make Gudrun welcome, hoping to persuade her to marry their son Hartmut. The young Norman princess, Ortrun, also offered her true friendship. But Gudrun said her heart was given to Herwig, and she could never love the man whose father had slain hers.

Queen Gerlint, believing Gudrun acted through pride, thought that harsh treatment might succeed where benevolence had failed. Gudrun and her women were set to servants' work, spinning and cleaning fires. Dressed in rags, Gudrun had to clean Gerlint's rooms three times each day using her own hair as a cloth, but still she did not yield.

Hartmut again offered to wed her, but she replied that she hated him and all his kin. "If you will not be my queen," said Hartmut, "I no longer care how anyone treats you."

Queen Gerlint then made Gudrun her washerwoman. Every day she had to carry heavy baskets of linen to the beach and wash them in the sea, with only one of her waiting women to help her. She bore this slavery for five years.

Eventually, Gudrun's mother, Queen Hilda of the Hegelings, decided to avenge her husband and rescue her daughter. Many knights were keen to help, especially Ortwin and Herwig, as well as Danes and Germans, including an old warrior named Wate. Siegfried of the Moors, remembering his love for Gudrun, joined them too.

Soon after, Gudrun, wearily scrubbing soiled clothes in the icy waves, was told by an angel in the shape of a bird that her kinsmen were coming; rejoicing, she neglected the washing, and was scolded for it.

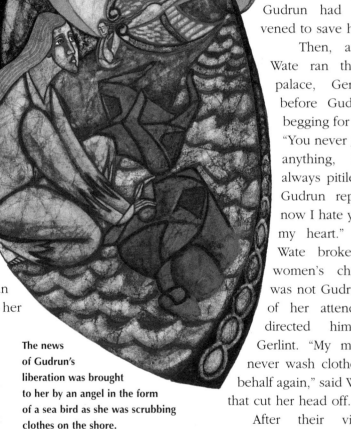

The news of Gudrun's liberation was brought to her by an angel in the form of a sea bird as she was scrubbing clothes on the shore.

Gudrun was barefoot and clad in rags when she looked up from her labour to see a boat bringing her own brother, Ortwin, and her beloved Herwig. Shamed by her appearance, she pretended, as the knights landed, to be a slave, but soon told the truth. Herwig would have carried her away immediately, but Ortwin insisted that they save all the women together, and they agreed to wait till the morrow.

Then Gudrun flung all Queen Gerlint's fine linen far out to sea, and strode back to the palace empty-handed. When Gerlint threatened to flog her, she falsely replied that she had changed her mind, and would indeed marry Hartmut. Nothing was too good for Gudrun and her women then, and Hartmut rejoiced.

At dawn, the Hegeling host attacked Ludwig's castle. A great battle followed, in which Herwig slew King Ludwig, avenging all those who had died earlier. Meanwhile, Hartmut would have been slain by Wate if Gudrun had not intervened to save his life.

Then, as enraged Wate ran through the palace, Gerlint knelt before Gudrun's feet, begging for protection. "You never granted me anything, but were always pitiless to me," Gudrun replied, "and now I hate you with all my heart." Yet when Wate broke into the women's chambers, it was not Gudrun but one of her attendants who directed him towards Gerlint. "My mistress will never wash clothes on your behalf again," said Wate, and at that cut her head off.

After their victory the Hegelings sailed home, taking Hartmut and Princess Ortrun prisoners; but later at Gudrun's request they were set free. Four marriages sealed the peace: Gudrun and Herwig, Ortwin and Ortrun, Siegfried the Moor and Herwig's sister, and Hartmut and Hildeburg, noblest of Gudrun's attendants. A tournament of many knights was organized, the guests exchanged lordly gifts, and friendship abounded.

99

Starkad, Hero and Traitor

One of the strangest legendary heroes was Starkad, known to both Saxo the Dane and the Icelandic saga writers, for he displayed the sternest heroic virtues yet was guilty of the most dishonourable crimes.

Starkad was a huge, misshapen man, with giants' blood in his veins; some said he had been born with eight arms, six of which Thor had torn off, while others claimed this had happened to his giant grandfather, not to him. Even without the extra arms he was hideous: "Ugly bald head, long snout, hair grey as a wolf's, dangling paws, crooked neck, wrinkled hide," as he put it himself.

Starkad's destiny was shaped by the favour of Odin and the enmity of Thor. Thor decreed he would be childless; Odin retorted that he would live three times as long as other men. Odin foretold he would have fine weapons, clothes and riches, and win every battle; Thor, that he would never own land, never think his riches great enough, and be wounded in each battle. It is not clear why Thor wished such evils on him, but it could well have been because of his giant ancestry; Thor always hated giants. For whatever reason, he was fated to commit three crimes.

Many sources describe Starkad's ferocity in battle and his scorn of all who were not fighters; he was the embodiment of the toughness and austerity of the Germanic ideal. He was also remembered as a poet, whose verses described the glories of war and his own victories. However, the most famous story about him is the tale of his first crime, committed against King Vikar (see page 32). Vikar's men decided to make a mock sacrifice of their king to Odin, and Starkad had to arrange it. To his dismay, the mock sacrifice became real and the king swung aloft to die by a twofold death, pierced and hanged at the same time. Starkad had paid homage to Odin, but at the cost of a treachery which filled him with shame, especially since Vikar had been his blood-brother – one of the most sacred bonds in the heroic code.

It is not explicitly stated in any of the old sources what Starkad's second crime was. Some scholars point to an occasion when he fled in battle, and others to the way he provoked tragic bloodshed at a young king's wedding by goading him into renewing a feud with his bride's family. This deed led to the deaths of all concerned – although Saxo praised the action.

The third crime was the murder of a king who trusted him. Acting on a bribe, Starkad cut the ruler's throat when he was naked and unarmed in his bath, though at first he dared not face his victim's piercing eyes. Once again, he was full of remorse after this deed.

At length, Starkad grew so old that he walked on two sticks, and was almost blind. He longed to die, but not in his bed; he wanted to perish by the sword, as a hero should. He hung his gold around his neck, hoping it might tempt some robber to kill him, but nobody dared attack him. Finally he taunted the son of one of the many men he had killed, jeering at him because he had not avenged his father; then he freely handed him his gold and his own sword as well. Thus encouraged, the younger man cut off Starkad's head. So at least Saxo tells the tale; but one poem says he died in a battle, and that his body went on fighting even after it had been beheaded. Either way, he was ferocious to the end, as befitted a hero whom Odin had befriended. No doubt a welcome awaited him in Valhalla, for he had served the god most faithfully, at great cost to himself and others.

Opposite: **Medieval ships from a Christian manuscript, c.AD1130. In the first of Starkad's heinous crimes he and a crew of men, becalmed off an island, effected a mock sacrifice in order to raise a wind and unwittingly killed their king.**

Grettir the Outlaw

"Great deeds and good luck are two different things," says an Icelandic proverb. The tale of Grettir the Strong shows how a man's bad luck could bring him to outlawry and a sordid death despite his courage. Written in the thirteenth century AD, it told the story of a luckless exile who supposedly died around AD1030, though it is doubtful whether he ever really existed.

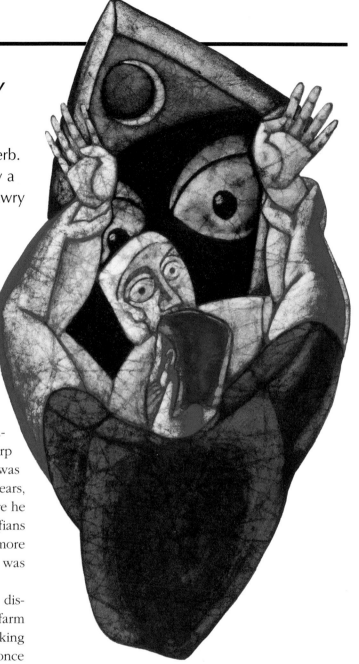

The ghoul Glam wrestles with his human adversary, Grettir. Sensing defeat, Glam inflicted on Grettir the curse that he would be haunted by the spectre of his ghastly staring eyes.

Grettir was the son of a rich Icelandic farmer who thought him stupid and lazy; in revenge, the boy would deliberately wreck any task that his father set him. He was unusually strong, quick to anger, and had a sharp tongue. So, when he killed a man, Grettir was blamed and banished to Norway for three years, although he had been unfairly provoked. There he found better outlets for his strength, killing ruffians or hunting bears. But he returned to Iceland more overbearing and self-confident than ever, and was soon embroiled in fresh feuds.

Grettir was always seeking new ways to display his strength. One day he heard of a farm plagued by a fearsome spook, one of the Walking Dead. This ghoul's name was Glam; he had once been a shepherd there. A big, grey-haired man with staring eyes, whom nobody much liked, he had been killed on the mountains by some ghost or troll. He then haunted the farm himself; night after night he attacked the livestock, and broke men's backs if they ventured outside.

Grettir offered to destroy Glam, though he was warned it would be dangerous to do so. Nevertheless he tackled the ghoul and sent him toppling backwards through the doorway of the farmhouse. Glam landed on his back in the courtyard, with Grettir on top of him. There was a bright moon, with light clouds drifting across it. As

Glam fell the moon shone forth, and he rolled his eyes up towards it. This was such a ghastly sight that Grettir's heart froze, and he lay transfixed with horror.

Then the dead man spoke: "You have worked hard to beat me, Grettir, but you will get little joy from it. From now on, everything you do will turn bad, and your luck will leave you – you will be outlawed. This is my curse on you: you will always see these eyes of mine before you, making it hard to live alone, which will cause your death."

Then Grettir's weakness passed, and he cut off Glam's head and burned the corpse to ashes. He rode home a changed man; he was rasher and more quick to anger than ever, but now he feared the dark so much that he dared not be alone at night, for Glam's eyes continually haunted him.

His bad luck soon began. Travelling in Norway again, he accidentally caused a fire in which two Icelanders died, and he was falsely called a murderer. Back in Iceland, the dead men's father became his enemy, and Grettir was outlawed, without a chance to defend himself.

Thus began long years of exile. He roamed from place to place in Iceland, sometimes finding a safe refuge for a while, but was always eventually forced to leave. He made many fresh enemies, and had many a narrow escape; he also sometimes fought against giants or she-trolls, and once passed the winter in a secret valley hidden among glaciers, kept warm by volcanic springs. But life there eventually became tedious, and he moved on.

At length he settled on an offshore islet called Drangey, with steep cliffs scaled by rope ladders. He had his brother Illugi with him, and a thrall, so that he need never face the dark alone. Sheep belonging to the mainland farmers grazed there, and seabirds abounded, so the living was good. But the farmers resented losing their sheep, and one of them rowed across to Drangey to complain; his old mother, reputed to be a witch, went with him. Grettir shouted from the cliffs that he would never leave the island, and in the ensuing quarrel the old woman cursed him, whereupon he hurled a rock into the boat, breaking her thigh. "I wish you had not done that," said Illugi.

Next spring this old woman hobbled down to the beach and found a big piece of driftwood. She cut runes on it, reddened them with her blood, and muttered something, walking widdershins around the log. Then her son pushed it into the sea and it drifted towards Drangey against the wind. Grettir's thrall gathered it as fuel, and as soon as Grettir tried to chop it, the axe glanced off

and sank into his right leg. The wound turned gangrenous, and soon the whole leg was festering.

So it was that when Grettir's enemies finally stormed Drangey they found him so sick he could not stand. Even so, he fought on his knees, killing one man, while Illugi killed three and wounded many more before he was overpowered. Then they closed in on Grettir to kill him, but he had already died from the gangrenous leg, so they cut off his head. They decided to kill Illugi too, at which he laughed, saying it was his only wish. The brothers were buried together on the island.

The story of Grettir the outlaw is set in the frozen expanses of Norway and Iceland, where the hostile landscapes made the ghoulish curse upon him all the more terrifying. The vision of the ghost's icy stare was to stay with Glam until his death.

Dietrich of Bern and his Champions

Theodoric the Great, like Charlemagne, was a ruler whose genuine historical achievements became gradually hidden in a haze of legend until his character was stripped down to that of the conventional figure of a noble and benevolent ruler, surrounded by valiant champions. But always the memory of glory clung to his name, which, in German sources, became "Dietrich of Bern", a corruption of Theodoric of Verona.

Theodoric became king of the Ostrogoths in AD474, at a time when this branch of the Gothic people were mercenaries serving the Emperor of Constantinople and living in Macedonia. In 488, with the emperor's approval, he led his people in a mass migration and invasion of northern Italy, where he defeated a ruler named Odoacer, besieging him for three years in Ravenna. Eventually Odoacer surrendered, but Theodoric treacherously killed him and established a kingdom of his own, which included the cities of Ravenna and Verona. There he reigned for thirty-three years, wisely and usually with justice, although he could be ruthless towards political enemies. He died in 526. Since he had been a heretical Arian Christian, not a Catholic, and since one of his political victims had been the Christian philosopher Boethius, medieval historians sometimes blackened his character.

So much for history. In legend, Dietrich's story is linked to those of major figures who in fact had died before he was even born: Ermenrich or Ermanaric, who killed himself in 375 when the Huns overran his kingdom, and Attila or Etzel the Hun, who died in 453. Legend claimed that Dietrich was the rightful heir to the Italian kingdom centred around Verona, which was usurped by Ermenrich (Odoacer's name is rarely

The character of Dietrich of Bern was based on the historical figure of Theodoric the Great. This mosaic (C.AD500), from the Church of Apollinare Nuovo, illustrates the grandeur of his palace in Ravenna, Italy.

The Wild Hunt

The forces of evil against which heroes sometimes had to contend could be heard in the howling gales of autumn and midwinter, when one might hear the clamour of a spectral hunt careering across the sky – hounds baying, horns echoing, the cries of the huntsmen and the screams of their prey.

The Wild Hunt, possibly inspired by the sound of wild geese crossing the sky, was greatly feared. To hear it was terrifying, but to see it brought bad luck or death, and prudent men would fling themselves face down onto the earth as it passed overhead.

In medieval times, it was said to be the Devil hunting damned souls, accompanied by a host of demons, hell-hounds and headless ghosts. Alternatively, there was a folk belief that the huntsman was intent on slaughtering wood-elves; or that the whole host of hunters were themselves a band of destructive spirits called the Oskorei.

When the Hunt had a single leader, the tales often identified him with some infamous king or

nobleman, or with a local landowner reputed to have lived an evil life. Intriguingly, the name "Oden" was given to the Huntsman in some parts of Sweden and Denmark; certainly the god Odin, leader of the dead and rider of a magical horse, might easily have been identified

The hunt took mythical dimensions in Germanic legend. This illumination is from an early 14th-century manuscript.

with such a figure as part of the Christian "demonization" of heathen gods, although leading the hunt was probably not one of his original attributes.

remembered). Driven into exile with a few follow-ers, Dietrich was warmly welcomed by Attila, in whose lands he remained for thirty years, until Ermenrich's death enabled him to reclaim his own kingdom. These stories originated among the Ostrogoths of northern Italy and passed from them to the Langobards; later they reached Bavaria and Austria, and spread throughout the Germanic and Scandinavian area.

Like Charlemagne or King Arthur, Dietrich is seen in medieval literature as a focal figure around whom other heroes gather – it is often their adventures which form the main topic of a poem, with the revered king remaining in the background. Alternatively, Dietrich may intervene decisively to bring some other heroes' conflict to a close, as he and his great warrior Hildibrand do in the final

stages of the Nibelung tragedy (see pages 94–5).

The earliest and most powerful tale from the Dietrich cycle is the German *Lay of Hildibrand*, a fragment dating from about AD800. Shortly before the battle in which Dietrich, after his long exile, would confront Odoacer to reclaim his kingdom, the old but doughty Hildibrand was standing guard at an outpost of the king's army. There he was challenged by a much younger warrior from the other host, and before agreeing to fight he demanded to know who this youth might be. From the reply it became clear to Hildibrand that it was Hadubrand, his own son, whom he had last seen as a baby before he followed Dietrich into exile thirty years before. But when Hildibrand made himself known, the younger man would not believe him, for he had been told his father was dead. Hildibrand then took a precious gold ring from his arm and offered it to his son, who replied: "Cunning old man, you seek to disarm me, but I shall give you my spear-point in exchange for that gift. You wear rich armour and gold rings; you are no wandering exile."

"Woe is me for my bitter fate," answered Hildibrand, "for either my own child shall kill me, or I shall have to kill him. As you praise my armour, come and get it; that should not be hard for you, from so old a man, if you have any strength or any right to it!"

But young Hadubrand merely insulted the old warrior with taunts of cowardice, and at length Hildibrand drew his sword; they fought, until both shields were splintered. At this point the story breaks off, but there can be no doubt from the tragic tone of the lay what the outcome was to be: the father, older but more experienced in warfare, would inevitably kill his own son.

The legends of Dietrich and his warriors were most fully recounted in the Norwegian *Thidrek's Saga*, compiled around AD1250 "from the tales and poems of German men", as its author declared. By then, the stark ferocity of Germanic epic had been largely replaced by the more diffuse and less tragic style that was fashionable in chivalric romances. It is typical that in this version Hildibrand's duel with his son ended in a mere wounding, followed by a reconciliation.

Various fantastic adventures were told of Dietrich in his youth. Thus, at twelve years old he was said to have obtained a wonderful sword from a dwarf whose life he had spared. Next, he and Hildibrand (who was also his foster-father) fought a robber-giant and his troll-like wife; the former was killed with ease, but the latter overpowered Hildibrand and bound him. Dietrich rushed to the rescue and cut the giantess in half, but she had such magic powers that the two halves rejoined again and again, until Hildibrand told Dietrich to set his foot between them, at which point she fell dead. Other tales told how Dietrich gathered

Known as "Sigurd's Helmet", this 7th-century headpiece is well-preserved and still has its chainmail intact. It may have belonged to Sigebert the Frank, a historical figure who died in AD575.

around him various heroic warriors, many of whom were famous in their own right. Such a relationship was usually formed after leader and follower had engaged in single combat in which each tested the other's skill on horseback and on foot, according to the rules of chivalry.

Once, Dietrich lost his way in a thick forest belonging to an evil lord called Ekka who slew everyone who entered it. Ekka waylaid Dietrich and challenged him to combat, boasting of his magnificent sword, the finest any dwarf ever made, with a gold hilt and scabbard and a blade so sharp that it seemed a snake went flashing up and down it from hilt to point and back again. The two foes sharpened their swords on the rocks till the sparks flew, and fought so fiercely that the forest seemed filled with lightning flashes and thunderclaps. Ekka at last struck Dietrich so hard that he fell to the ground, and he would have taken him captive, except that Dietrich's horse, seeing his master's danger, bit through his tether and broke Ekka's back with a blow from his hooves. Then Dietrich cut off his head and took his armour and weapons, which he put on instead of his own. Thus disguised, he encountered a certain Fasold, brother to Ekka, but after an inconclusive combat the two swore friendship. Together they encountered other adventures, killing an elephant (again with help from Dietrich's horse), and rescuing a warrior named Sistram, who had been half swallowed by a dragon. Fasold and Sistram rode back to Verona with Dietrich, and joined his household.

While Dietrich's fame, wealth and glory increased, his uncle Ermenrich was making himself overlord of Rome and of many other realms in Italy, the Balkans and Greece. But Ermenrich, unlike Dietrich, was a cruel and grasping man, and was much influenced by a counsellor even more evil than himself, whose name is given as Bikka in some tales, and as Sifka in others. By cunning lies and plots, this man tricked King Ermenrich into killing many of those closest to him, among them his wife, his son and his nephews. (Some say Sifka's motive was a desire for vengeance because Ermenrich had once raped his wife.) Moreover, he

This 11th-century brooch from Iceland employs a snake motif. Many Viking weapons and jewels took their decorative inspiration from serpents, which in the narrative of Dietrich symbolized speed and deadliness.

urged Ermenrich to claim tribute from kings who in fact owed him none. Among these was Dietrich; and when Dietrich refused, Ermenrich attacked Verona and drove him into exile.

After some years had passed, Dietrich, accompanied by many of his champions and by the sons of his friend and ally Etzel the Hun, made war on Ermenrich in the hope of reconquering his kingdom. The attempt failed, partly as a result of a jealous rivalry which broke out between two of Dietrich's finest champions, Vidia and Hama.

Vidia ended up by defecting to Ermenrich's host, while Hama decided to remain loyal to Dietrich. Vidia then slew Dietrich's brother in

107

battle, although unwillingly. When Dietrich pursued him, intent on vengeance, he galloped into the sea and drowned rather than turn face the master he had betrayed.

Returning to his kingdom once Ermenrich was dead, Dietrich reigned long and prosperously. There are not many legends about his death, which in historical fact was a natural one. One near-contemporary, the Byzantine historian Procopius, claimed that he died of a fever brought on by the shock of seeing in the head of a fish served to him at a banquet a resemblance to the scowling face of a man he had unjustly sentenced to death. A later chronicler reported that at the moment of Dietrich's death, a hermit had a vision of his soul being bound and dragged by two of his victims to the crater of Etna, popularly thought to be an entrance to Hell.

In the course of time, other legends sprang up. One was that Vidia did not perish at sea but was pulled from death by a mermaid, and that he and Dietrich subsequently confronted one another in a final duel. In it the king slew Vidia but received grievous wounds from which he died shortly afterwards. As he was dying, he went to a nearby lake and hurled his sword as far out into

A legend tells how Vidia, one of Dietrich's champions, nearly drowned but was saved from death by a mermaid. More commonly, mermaids, shown here in a 15th-century manuscript illumination, were thought to lure victims to a watery grave.

the water as he was able, so that no man could ever use the weapon after him.

But others said that one day Dietrich was in his bath when a pageboy ran in and told him that a magnificent stag had been seen nearby. The king, who dearly loved hunting, shouted for his horse and hounds, but there was some delay in bringing his mount. As he waited impatiently, he noticed another horse, a large black one, standing already saddled, and leapt onto its back.

The beast galloped off at an incredible speed, and the king's men could not keep pace with it. Then Dietrich, knowing something was amiss, tried to dismount, but found he was stuck to the charger's back. "Why do you ride so fast, my lord?" cried one of his men. "An evil ride," Dietrich answered, "for this is no horse, but a devil. Yet I shall return one day, if it is the will of God and Blessed Mary." The horse then vanished, and from that day to this nobody can say what became of King Dietrich.

How the Lombards Came to Italy

Lombardy, that part of northern Italy between the Alps and the Po, was for centuries a disputed land, fought over by Romans, Byzantines and Ostrogoths; in AD568 it was invaded by the Germanic tribe who called themselves the "Langobards" (later, "Lombards"). They ruled it for 200 years, until overthrown by Charlemagne.

According to their own tales, the Langobards were originally called the Vinils, and lived on the islands of Denmark in the 2nd and 3rd centuries AD. They became so numerous that the land could no longer support them, so to avert famine their king decreed that one third of the population must be killed or exiled. Lots were drawn, and those on whom the lot fell emigrated to seek a new home in foreign lands. They were led by two brothers, Ibor and Ayo, and their mother Gambara.

The Vinils first came to Skoringen, an area south of the Baltic, where they lived peacefully for some years, until a nearby tribe, the ferocious Vandals, demanded tribute from them. Ibor and Ayo refused, preferring to fight for freedom rather than to become tributaries. The night before the battle, the Vandals prayed to Woden for victory, and the god, who favoured them, replied: "I shall grant victory to those I see first at sunrise."

Gambara, mother of the Vinil leaders, also prayed – in her case to Freyja – for victory. The goddess advised her to have all the Vinil women stand on the battlefield alongside their menfolk, with their hair drawn forward about their jaws like beards. Then Freyja turned Woden's bed around while he slept, so that when he looked onto the battlefield at dawn he faced the Vinils, not the Vandals. He cried out in surprise: "Who are those longbeards?" To this Freyja replied: "When a name is given, a gift goes with it, so you must grant them victory." And so the Vinils won, and thenceforth called themselves Langobards, or "Long Beards".

The rugged terrain of Lombardy. The land was conquered in the 6th century by the Langobards who had been forced to migrate from Denmark around AD250 because of overpopulation.

How Alboin Obtained a Sword

Mere prowess in battle was not enough proof of valour for the Langobards. Alboin, who was to settle his people by conquest in Northern Italy, had to prove himself in his youth by an act of courage that bordered on effrontery.

In his youth, Alboin had fought successfully in his people's war against the Gepids, and had killed their prince, Thurismod. Returning home, the warriors asked that Alboin should sit in honour at the table of his father, King Audoin, during the victory feast. But Audoin refused him this privilege, saying it was a Langobard custom not to let a prince eat at his father's table until he had managed to obtain a sword from a foreign king.

Hearing this, Alboin at once rode off with forty young companions to the stronghold of Thurisend, King of the Gepids, where he claimed hospitality as a peaceful guest. Thurisend could not in honour refuse; he welcomed the Langobards to his banqueting hall, and seated Alboin at his side, where his dead son Thurismod used to sit, although he knew well that it was by Alboin's hand that Thurismod had met his death. As the young prince took his place, Thurisend sighed: "That seat is dear to me, a grief to me is he who now sits there!"

Others among his entourage were less patient. One of the king's younger sons mocked the Langobards because they wore white leggings: "You look like white-legged mares – have many men ridden you?" To this one of the Langobards retorted: "You there, whose prince's bones lie scattered on the meadow like those of a wretched old pack-horse, go back to the battlefield, and learn how hard these mares can kick!"

Both sides reached for their weapons. But King Thurisend put himself between them and ordered his followers to keep the peace, saying it would be an offence to God to attack guests in one's own hall. Thus he calmed the potential strife, and after the feast he took the sword which had belonged to Thurismod, and gave it to Alboin with his very own hands.

Then Alboin triumphantly returned home to his father, and was granted a seat at his table. When he told what had happened among the Gepids, the Langobards marvelled at Alboin's boldness, and at Thurisend's great wisdom and magnanimity.

A gold and iron sword c.AD1000 of the type used by the Vikings, inscribed with its owner's name.

Wandering south through Burgundy, Moravia and Austria, the Langobards faced many enemies. In some cases, they won new territories by open warfare, in others by trickery, and on at least one occasion by single combat, as when their leader Lamissio fought a duel with the champion of a race of warrior maidens. Sometimes they used magic; once they created the illusion that a field of flax was a lake, so that their enemies spread their arms and tried to swim across it. In this unfortunate posture they were easily struck down by the Langobards' swords.

In AD565 Alboin succeeded his father as king of the Langobards, who were by then settled in Pannonia (part of the Roman Empire corresponding to western Hungary). By that time he was already a famous warrior, renowned for his victory over the Gepids (see opposite). Three years later he led a migration into Italy, where he won extensive territories, ruling at Pavia until his death in 573. It is said that his glorious deeds were told in songs, not only by the Langobards but by Bavarians, Saxons and other Germanic peoples.

Alboin's death was due to his old enmity with the Gepids. So long as King Thurisend was alive there was peace between them and the Langobards, but his son and successor, Kunimund, renewed the war. However, Alboin defeated him, killed him with his own hands, and then had a drinking-cup made out of his skull. He also captured Kunimund's daughter, Rosimund, and later made her his wife. One day, in a merry mood, Alboin told his queen to serve wine in the cup made from her father's skull, and drink from it herself. "Drink cheerfully with your father!" he said.

Rosimund resented this bitterly but hid her feelings, and plotted revenge. She persuaded a young warrior called Peredeo to assassinate Alboin. To ensure her husband's death, Rosimund took his sword and tied it to the bedpost so that it could not be drawn from its scabbard. Then she let Peredeo in, and when attacked Alboin found he could not use his sword to defend himself. He died, a victim of his wife's cunning.

Rosimund was forced by her husband, Alboin, to drink wine from a cup made from her father's skull. She pretended not to mind, but prepared to take revenge later.

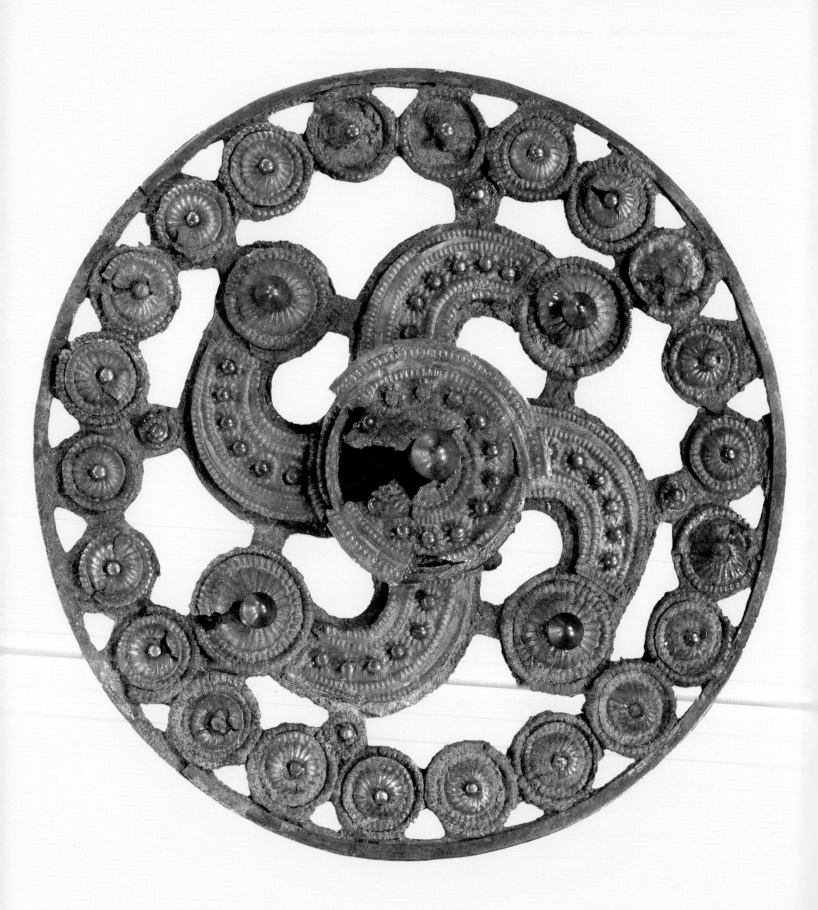

CREATION AND THE DOOM OF THE GODS

The concept of an inescapable fate was deeply embedded in the whole of Norse mythology, for the myths told of a future catastrophe, Ragnarok, in which gods and mankind would be entirely destroyed. Although it lay in the future, its every detail was described with the same certainty as if it had already taken place. The Norse people imagined the creation of the world, its cosmology and its inevitable final destruction, as a single unit in a continuing cycle of creations, each of which ended in an apocalypse before the world was renewed. Humans fitted into this cosmic scheme as one of several types of beings, each group contributing to the life of the others. But although they cohabited with gods, dwarves, animals and giants, people were powerless to influence fate and change the course of events. The end of the world was inherent in its very beginning: its doom was conceived even as the shape and form of the world was revealed.

Life began in the fusion of two elemental extremes, ice and fire, and was doomed to end when flames and water would once again engulf all that had been engendered. A chain of episodes, expedited by the rancorous Loki, was to end in a final confrontation in which the forces of chaos and evil would be pitted against the gods, and each side would destroy the other in the dramatic finale known as Ragnarok. But like the ancient whirling wheel, a symbol commonly found on Viking picture stones, the cycle would turn again.

The catastrophe was to be triggered by the death of Balder, son of Odin and Frigg, who was considered the purest of the gods and the most popular among them. Yet he was destined to return to life afterwards and preside over a newly-created, more peaceful world. For, having purged the earth of evil, Ragnarok would lead to the regeneration of life: the earth would reappear from the waters of chaos, washed clean and made anew.

Yggdrasill, the ash tree that was guardian and protector of the universe and absorber of its stresses and woes, was foreordained to remain standing throughout the onslaught of the final battle. In its eternal branches it sheltered a man and a woman – Lif and Lifthrasir – who would become the first of a new generation of humans, destined to people the earth again.

This Bronze Age gold brooch, found in a grave in Denmark, incorporates the symbolic turning wheel, which may represent the sun moving across the sky. Norse creation and apocalypse myths are cyclical; the end of the world ushers in a new beginning.

Below: A cast silver pendant (*c.*AD900) possibly depicting a Valkyrie, chooser of the slain warriors who dwelt in Valhalla.

The Creation of the Universe

Norse creation myths were permeated by the natural elements that were regular features of the people's environment. The engendering of life, the formation of the cosmos, and the establishment of the heavenly bodies were all seen as determined by the dramatic collision of heat with cold, most vividly typified by volcanic activity in a sub-arctic landscape.

The most important sources for Norse beliefs about creation are the thirteenth-century poems *Voluspa*, *Grimnismal* and *Vafthrudnismal*, which the Icelandic chronicler Snorri Sturluson translated and expanded upon from other varied sources not now known to us in his detailed account in the *Prose Edda*.

As Snorri tells it, at the beginning of time, before the earth had been formed, there was nothing in existence – just a gaping void called Ginnungagap. To the south of this was Muspell, an impassable region which was bright, burning hot and full of flames. Freezing cold Niflheim (which later became the land of the dead) lay to the north. In the midst of Niflheim was Hvergelmir, a spring from which flowed eleven rivers collectively

known as Elivagar. As these rivers flowed away from their source, the poisonous lees that they deposited began to harden and turned to ice. When the ice came to a halt the vapour rising from the poison froze into rime, layer upon layer, until it had spread right across Ginnungagap.

Grim cold now emanated from Niflheim and that part of Ginnungagap that faced northwards, but the southernmost part was warmed by the sparks and hot wind that blew out of Muspell. As the rime met the hot gusts it melted, and from the moisture life began.

A sense of foreboding, struggle and hostility pervades Norse creation myths, reflecting the harsh environment typified by this Norwegian landscape.

Light Elves, Dark Elves and Dwarves

Dwarves and elves had widely differing roles, yet both groups added a further dimension to the mythology and lives of the Scandinavian peoples. Dwarves were associated with the gods and fashioned their magical treasures, whereas elves affected the lives of mortals, causing nightmares and diseases.

Dwarves were master craftsmen and particularly skilful smiths, able to fashion extraordinary objects to which they gave marvellous properties. They were the creators of most of the treasures belonging to the gods, including Mjollnir, Thor's hammer; Draupnir, Odin's ring; Freyja's famous necklace; Sif's hair and Freyr's golden boar as well as his ship Skidbladnir (see page 43). They also made Gleipnir, the only fetter that was able to restrain the monstrous wolf Fenrir (see page 55) and brewed the precious mead of poetry (see page 29).

Occasionally, when dwarves were forced to forge treasures against their will, or were made to give them up, they would place curses upon them. The gold wrested by Sigurd from the dragon Fafnir was originally taken by Loki from a dwarf, who then laid a curse that caused the downfall of the Volsungs (see pages 90–91).

The race of dwarves was thought to have been generated from the soil. Snorri tells how they first took form as maggots in the flesh of Ymir, a primeval giant whose huge body was made into the earth, and were then given consciousness and intelligence by the gods. They lived underground or in rocks, sometimes under mountains, and with their love of gold and

This carved-stone relief decorating a 12th-century Swedish baptismal font depicts a dwarf hard at work at his forge.

other precious metals and stones they were on occasion envisaged as miners.

The poem *Alvissmal* tells of a particularly wise dwarf, Alviss, who came to Asgard while Thor was away and persuaded the Aesir to give him Thor's daughter as his bride. Thor met him as he was hurrying home with her, and was greatly displeased. He apprehended Alviss, but slyly promised to consent to the marriage if the dwarf could answer all the

questions he chose to put to him. The wise dwarf managed to answer fully but Thor continued to quiz him all night long. Dwarves can only survive in the dark, and when the first rays of sunlight hit him, Alviss turned to stone.

Elves – supernatural beings of lesser stature than gods – figured in most Germanic mythology. They were known to the Western Germanic peoples and the Anglo-Saxons, and they were an accepted part of the general cosmology. They even appear sometimes to have been worshipped by the population.

There were two types of elves in Norse myth. Light elves, thought to be more beautiful than the sun, lived in Alfheim, on the same level of the world as Asgard. Dark elves, who were blacker than pitch, lived underground in Midgard.

Across the Germanic regions elves were associated with the land and nature. An Anglo-Saxon word meaning "pretty as an elf" attests to their perceived beauty and allure, but they were also considered potentially dangerous. In Anglo-Saxon England elves were thought to cause disease, nightmares even and hiccups. Other illnesses, associated by name with elves, are also found in Norway and Iceland, showing that such beliefs were widespread.

The World Tree

The axis of the universe was an enormous ash tree, Yggdrasill, also known as the World Tree, which formed a column linking the worlds of the gods, mankind, the giants and the dead. Its fortunes mirrored those of the universe it sheltered; as well as sustaining the world, it suffered in the same way as those who dwelt in it.

The world tree, Yggdrasill, was constantly gnawed by deer and other creatures, as depicted in this Viking-Age carving from Urnes, Norway.

Nothing is known of the origin of Yggdrasill. It appears to have been timeless, existing before the beginning of the world and destined to survive Ragnarok.

A variety of creatures dwelt in or by the tree: a wise eagle who sat in its uppermost branches, with a hawk called Vedrfolnir between its eyes; a monstrous serpent, Nidhogg, who lay deep down in Niflheim, by its roots; a squirrel named Ratatosk who ran up and down its trunk carrying insults between the eagle and the serpent; and four stags, named Dain, Dvalin, Duneyr and Durathror, who lived among the tree's branches eating young green shoots. To them and others the tree was a source of life. It dripped dew so sweet that bees made honey from it, and its cooked fruit was said to be helpful to women in labour, hastening the emergence of the child.

As well as providing protection and nourishment for the world, the tree was said to suffer anguish and bitter hardships, caused by the very creatures it sustained. The stags and squirrel stripped it of new growth, and Nidhogg gnawed at its roots, as did countless other serpents. In this way the tree knew the tribulations of the universe at every level and suffered just as much as those who dwelt in it.

To counteract this damage and pain, the Norns (see page 121), who dwelt by the well of Urd, tended the tree every day by pouring water and mud from the well over the branches so they would not rot away. The water was so holy that everything it touched immediately turned as white as the delicate film inside an eggshell.

As guardian to the whole world, Yggdrasill was the supreme example of a widespread belief in trees' protective qualities. In Germany, Scandinavia and the British Isles, particular trees beside buildings were venerated, and the welfare of the family or community was seen to depend on their health. Offerings were made to them; for example, ale was poured over their roots.

Temples also had guardian trees: Adam of Bremen, in his description of the temple at Uppsala, refers to a great evergreen growing close at hand. Details of his description are remarkably similar to those of Yggdrasill in Norse poetry: the tree's broad outstretched branches offered shelter to the temple, and there was a sacred well at its foot.

The melting drops initially formed a giant, Ymir, from whom a race of frost-giants descended. The first of these were created while Ymir slept: he sweated, and under his left armpit grew a male and a female, while one of his legs begot a monstrous giant son on the other.

Further melting ice created a cow called Audhumla. Four rivers of milk flowed from her udder, and these fed Ymir. For her own sustenance Audhumla licked the salty rime stones. On the first day, as she licked, a man's hair became visible, on the second day a man's head emerged, and by the end of the third day a complete man was in existence. Life thus grew originally out of a convergence of polarities – the reaction of heat and cold on one another.

The man that Audhumla licked from the salty ice-blocks was strong, handsome and of great stature. Named Buri, he begot a son called Bor, who married Bestla, the daughter of a frost-giant called Bolthorn. They produced three sons: the gods Odin, Vili and Ve, who in time decided to kill the primeval giant Ymir. So much blood flowed from his wounds when he fell that the whole race of frost-giants was drowned except for one, known as Bergelmir. He escaped and became the progenitors of a new race of giants.

The Origins of the World and of People

Odin and his brothers then created the world out of Ymir. They carried his body out into the middle of Ginnungagap and made the earth out of his flesh and formed rocks from his bones. They fashioned stones and gravel from his teeth and shattered bones, and with the blood flowing from his wounds they created lakes and the sea. From Ymir's skull they formed the sky and set it up over the earth, placing four dwarves, Nordri, Sudri, Austri and Vestri (who represented North, South, East and West) at each corner to hold it up. To create flora, the gods used Ymir's hair. Finally, they threw his brains into the sky to form the clouds.

The three gods took sparks and glowing particles that were flying out of Muspell and set them

Cattle clearly played an important role in the lives as well as the mythology of the early Scandinavian peoples, for whom a cow helped create humanity. This Bronze-Age rock carving comes from Bohuslan in western Sweden.

in the firmament both above and below the earth to become the stars in the sky. They gave positions to all of them, and ordained their courses. Some were fixed, while others moved in a wandering fashion around and below the earth they had constructed. The earth itself was circular, and they placed a vast sea around it. Along the shore they allotted land to the giants, while inland they made a fortification against them out of Ymir's eyelashes, within which lay Midgard, the realm the human race was to inhabit.

Once the world had been established, the gods created people to live in it. As Odin and his brothers walked along the sea shore, they came upon two tree trunks and created a man and a woman from them. Odin gave the new beings breath and life, Vili gave them consciousness and movement, and Ve gave each a face, speech, hearing and sight. (*Voluspa* gives a slightly different account, stating that the trio that gave humans these attributes were Odin and the gods Honir and Lodur.) The man was named Ask ("ash tree") and the woman Embla (possibly meaning "elm", or "vine"). From them descended all those who lived in Midgard.

The credit for creating the different social classes goes to the god Heimdall (see page 129), an enigmatic figure about whom little is known but who must have been important within the Norse pantheon. One day Heimdall came to a farmhouse which he entered, disguising himself under the pseudonym Rig. There he was received by a couple, Ai and Edda ("great-grandfather" and "great-grandmother") who gave him coarse, heavy bread and beef broth to eat. At nightfall they invited him to rest with them, and he remained there for three days, sharing the couple's bed each night. Nine months after his departure, Edda gave birth to a son, a swarthy child with dark hair and dull eyes. Named Thrall, he was condemned to spend his life performing hard manual labour. He married an equally unattractive woman. From them descended the race of slaves.

Heimdall, again introducing himself as Rig, came to another house, where he was received by a couple called Afi and Amma ("grandfather" and "grandmother"). This couple were more affluent. They had wooden floors in their house and they were well-presented: their hair was combed and they were smartly dressed. Rig was entertained with a trencher full of meat, and once again stayed with this couple for three nights, sleeping between them. Nine months later Amma in her turn gave birth to a son. Called Karl ("freeman"), he had a ruddy complexion and bright eyes. He grew up to build houses and to farm land, and from him the race of free men was descended.

Rig finally came to the home of a third couple, Fadir and Modir ("father" and "mother"), who were expensively dressed and lived in luxury. Modir laid out a sumptuous meal of bread, meat, poultry and wine, and entertained her guest royally. As usual, Rig stayed for three nights, sleeping between the couple as before. In nine months a boy was born, who was named Jarl ("earl"). He had flaxen hair and a fair complexion, and his eyes glittered like jewels.

Jarl grew up accomplished in all aristocratic pursuits; he was particularly skilled in the use of a bow, spear and sword, in riding, hunting and swimming. Heimdall eventually acknowledged him as his own son and taught him knowledge of the runes. Jarl became rich, and was married to a beautiful woman. The nobility descended from their children.

More than half a metre long, the Trundholm chariot dates from the Bronze Age. Day was believed to be driven across the sky in such a chariot by Sun.

Fire, Ice and Water

Although particular, recognizable places do not feature in the Norse stories of the origin of the world, specific sites or natural features can be identified which may have provided the inspiration for important aspects of the creation myths.

It was in Iceland that most of the myths took the shape in which they have survived until today. The idea of intense heat meeting cold to generate life could well have originated in a place where this unusual juxtaposition is commonly seen: Iceland's ice-covered volcanoes erupt, spewing out boiling lava, flames and steam, and the ice caps melt flooding the valleys below.

Other elements of the creation myths may be associated with a place that the Roman historian Tacitus described as holy to the Germans. At the salt springs of the River Saale, near Strassfurt, people obtained salt by pouring water over piles of burning wood. Tacitus noted that this process involved uniting two opposing elements, water and fire, thereby apparently presenting the same conditions that engendered life in the story of Audhumla.

Night and Day

While creating the universe, the gods also organized the cycle of night and day and the passage of time – the days, weeks, months and seasons. They did this by enlisting the aid of a giantess called Night, who was black and dark. She had three husbands, the last of whom, Delling, was of the race of the Aesir. Their son was called Day, and he was bright and fair, like his father. Odin took Night and Day and placed them in horsedrawn chariots up in the sky to ride around the earth every twenty-four hours. Night was drawn by a horse called Hrimfaxi ("Rime-mane"), who bedewed the earth with drips from his bit. Day's horse, called Skinfaxi ("Shining-mane"), lit up the sky and the earth with his luminous mane.

A man called Mundilfari had a son and a daughter whom he thought so beautiful that he named them Sun and Moon. Angry at such presumption, the gods stole away the children and put them in the sky to drive the chariots of their own son and daughter.

The sun and the moon moved fast on their journey, for two wolves, descended from the offspring of an ancient giantess who lived in a forest called Jarnvid ("Ironwood") east of Midgard, perpetually chased them. The one that pursued the sun was called Skoll, and he was destined to catch her (see page 130). Running ahead of the sun, trying to catch the moon, (which he too would do one day) was a wolf called Hati Hrodvitnisson.

The Three Levels of Existence

The cosmology of the Norse mythological world as it emerges from the later myths is not easy to reconcile with that depicted in the creation stories, and it is certainly impossible to draw up a precise map using evidence from them. The best that can be done is to paint an impressionistic portrait of varied landscapes and vast distances. But then, even in the real world, topographical accuracy was not a prime concern of the Vikings.

Yggdrasill

ASGARD
Realm of the Aesir

The Well
of Urd

VANAHEIM
Land of the Vanir

VALHALLA
Hall of the Slain

Bifrost

The Well
of Mimir

MIDGARD

JOTUNHEIM
Land of the Giants

The World Serpent,
Jormungand

Spring of
Hvergelmir

NIFLHEIM
World of the Dead

HEL

The Dragon, Nidhogg

The creation myths present a flat world, with Asgard, Midgard and Jotunheim all on one level surrounded by the sea. In all other Norse myths, however, the world seems to consist of three different levels, stacked one above the other like a series of plates. On top was Asgard, where the gods lived in their magnificent halls, as well as Vanaheim, abode of the Vanir, and Alfheim, the home of the light elves. Here too, lived those who died in battle, feasting in Odin's hall, Valhalla, or Freyja's hall, Sessrumnir. On the level below was Midgard, the world of men, and Jotunheim, the mountainous land of the giants. The underground homes of the dwarves and the dark elves were also located here.

Asgard and Midgard were connected by the flaming bridge Bifrost, which appears to mortals as the rainbow. Snorri describes it as very strong, with three colours, and says that it was built with more skill than any other structure.

Down below on the third level, was Niflheim, world of the dead, which included Hel, where those who died of sickness, old age or accident were judged. It was named after its guardian, Loki's monstrous daughter.

The different worlds were linked by the central column of the World Tree, the great ash

In the Norse creation stories the world appears to be flat, but in other myths it was divided into three levels, Asgard (home to the gods), Midgard (where humans, dwarves and giants dwelt) and Niflheim (the realm of the dead). All were linked by Yggdrasill whose roots penetrated each level.

Yggdrasill, whose three roots reached all three levels and whose branches extended above them all providing shelter and sustenance. One root was embedded in Asgard, under which was the well of Urd (fate) where the gods held their council every day. The second root delved into Jotunheim, and sheltered the well of Mimir, the repository of wisdom where Odin was to leave one of his eyes in return for a knowledge-giving drink. The third root extended down into Niflheim, and beneath it was the spring of Hvergelmir, the source of the rivers that contributed to the world's creation.

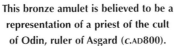

This bronze amulet is believed to be a representation of a priest of the cult of Odin, ruler of Asgard (c.AD800).

Various stories of the gods' travels give an impression of the distances and type of terrain thought to lie between each world. Hermod's journey from Asgard to Hel (see page 126) takes him nine nights downwards and northwards, through valleys full of darkness and over almost impassable mountains and rivers. The road from Asgard to Jotunheim led eastwards, and it was necessary to cross the ocean in a boat and then, on land again, to navigate huge forests before reaching it. Thor made this journey regularly. For example, he planned a journey to Utgard in the summer, so that he could test himself against the giants (see pages 42–46).

The Norns, Shapers of Destiny

Norns were female supernatural figures who were thought to determine the destinies of individuals. Three particular Norns lived by the well of Urd, but there were other Norns as well, both benevolent and malevolent, who could reverse a person's fortune at their whim.

Of the three principal Norns who lived by the well of Urd (fate), situated beneath one of the roots of Yggdrasill, one was actually named Urd, while the others were Verdandi ("being") and Skuld ("necessity"). They were said to determine the lives of men and allot their lifespans. According to *Voluspa*, they "cut on wood", which may refer to the action of carving magical runes. However, the Viking word for wood also refers to a large plank, and it was customary in Norway to record dates and numbers of days and years by cutting notches into the wooden walls of the home. So this term may just mean that they recorded the days in an individual's life.

Other Norns were thought to visit each child as it was born to determine events in its life. A runic inscription found in a church in Borgund in Norway reads: "The Norns determine good and bad things and they have brought great sorrow to me." These Norns differed in their origins. Some were divine, some were of the race of elves, some were of the race of dwarves. An individual's fortune and quality of life were explained by the origins of the Norn that was believed to protect him or her. Good Norns, of divine lineage, were thought to influence lives favourably, but misfortune was associated with malevolent Norns, thought to descend from baser ancestry.

Norns were also sometimes pictured allotting destiny by spinning: in the poem *Helgakvida Hundingsbana* (The Lay of Helgi, the Slayer of Hunding) the Norns are depicted spinning and weaving the threads of Helgi's fate.

SACRIFICE AND BURIAL

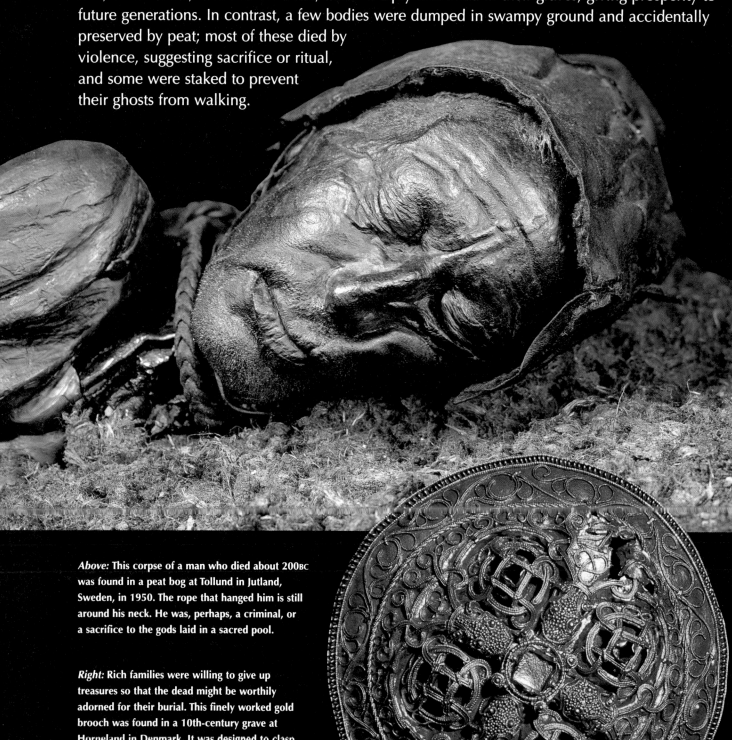

Throughout the Germanic world, the dead were honoured by careful burial or cremation, often with valuable possessions to accompany them into the afterlife; moreover, their mounds or stones were raised in conspicuous places. Some people were thought to go to Valhalla, Odin's hall, or Niflheim, realm of the dead; others simply remained in their graves, giving prosperity to future generations. In contrast, a few bodies were dumped in swampy ground and accidentally preserved by peat; most of these died by violence, suggesting sacrifice or ritual, and some were staked to prevent their ghosts from walking.

Above: This corpse of a man who died about 200BC was found in a peat bog at Tollund in Jutland, Sweden, in 1950. The rope that hanged him is still around his neck. He was, perhaps, a criminal, or a sacrifice to the gods laid in a sacred pool.

Right: Rich families were willing to give up treasures so that the dead might be worthily adorned for their burial. This finely worked gold brooch was found in a 10th-century grave at Horneland in Denmark. It was designed to clasp together a man's cloak.

Right: Traditionally, the Vikings practised both common types of burial: cremation and inhumation. Even humble graves would have been marked by stones, which sometimes formed the outline of a ship. This burial site, at Aalborg in North Jutland, Denmark, shows evidence of multiple interments.

Above: The grave may have been thought of as a home, or a bed. Here a man lies snug in a wooden chamber, resting on cushions. With him are his neck-ring, sword and shield. The corpse, found in Denmark, was probably buried during the early Bronze Age (1500–800BC).

Right: From a Viking woman's grave at Nornelund, near Varde, Denmark, two oval brooches, which held the shoulder-straps of her dress, are linked by a string of cornelian, crystal and glass beads. The smaller trefoil brooch was worn on the the chest, probably to fasten a shawl.

The Death of Balder

The death of Balder is probably the most famous of all the Norse myths. The event underlines the mortality of the gods and the limits on their power. Even Odin, who journeys to the land of the dead to discover Balder's fate, is unable to prevent the tragedy. Balder, the most beautiful and beloved of the Aesir, is the victim of malice, and his demise is the harbinger of far worse destruction; it indicates that evil has come among the gods. Their ultimate destruction in Ragnarok cannot be far away.

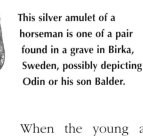

This silver amulet of a horseman is one of a pair found in a grave in Birka, Sweden, possibly depicting Odin or his son Balder.

When the young and noble god Balder had a series of nightmares, the gods thought them to be omens. Hearing this news, Odin decided to saddle up Sleipnir and ride to Niflheim to discover the meaning of the dreams. He sought the grave of a long-dead seeress. When he found it, he chanted spells that forced her against her will to rise up and speak to him about the future of the gods. She told Odin that Hel was preparing for Balder's arrival and that the blind god, Hod, was destined to be his unwitting killer. Sensing the ominous implications of her prophecies, Odin rode home with a heavy heart.

The Aesir met together to discuss this devastating news, for it was of great concern to them. Balder's mother, Frigg, decided to safeguard her son by extracting solemn oaths from all things animate and inanimate not to harm him. When this had been done, the Aesir amused themselves by persuading Balder to stand before their assemblies while they playfully threw things at him, knowing that none could harm him.

Loki grew jealous and conceived a plan. Changing himself into a woman he went to visit Frigg at her home, Fensalir. Frigg asked the woman if she knew what the Aesir were doing. The visitor replied that they were shooting at Balder, but he was not being hurt. "Neither weapons nor wood will harm Balder. I have received oaths from all things," said Frigg. The woman then asked if indeed every single thing in existence had sworn an oath not to hurt Balder, and Frigg replied that one plant, a small tree called mistletoe growing to the west of Valhalla, had seemed to her too young to make such a vow.

With this in mind, Loki went in search of the mistletoe, pulled it up and took it to the assembly. Restored to his usual form, he approached Hod, who was standing alone outside the circle of gods. Loki asked him why he was not shooting at Balder. "Because I cannot see him," replied Hod, "and I have no weapon." "I will direct your aim if you want to shoot at him with this stick," said Loki.

Hod took aim as the trickster directed. When the stick hit Balder it pierced him through and he fell down dead. This was said to be the unluckiest deed ever performed among gods and men. When the Aesir saw what had happened they were speechless with shock and could only weep. They were all certain that Loki was responsible for the death, but they could not punish him — it was forbidden to spill blood on assembly ground.

Frigg eventually formed a plan. She sought a volunteer to ride to Niflheim to offer Hel a ransom

Opposite: **Balder died at the hands of the blind god Hod, who was tricked into shooting him with mistletoe. This drawing by Olafur Brynjulfsson illustrated a medieval version of the *Edda*.**

for Balder's release. Hermod, Balder's brother, came forward and agreed to go on Odin's horse Sleipnir. When he got to Hel she told him that the strength of feeling for Balder must be tested before she would release him: "If all things in the world will weep for Balder, then I will let him go."

When Hermod arrived back at Asgard and relayed Hel's condition to the Aesir, they sent messengers all over the world to ensure that Balder should be wept out of Hel. Everyone and everything complied, except a giantess called Thokk (thought to be Loki in disguise), who refused, saying, "Thokk will weep dry tears for Balder. I had nothing good from him dead or alive."

After this Loki ran away and hid on a mountain, where he built a house with four doors so that he could keep watch on all sides. By day he transformed himself into a salmon and sheltered beneath a waterfall. At night, sitting in his house, he wondered what sort of device the Aesir might use to catch him and laced together some twine, thereby inventing the first fishing net.

Then Loki noticed through one of the doors that the Aesir were nearby. He immediately threw the net into the fire, and rushed to the river. However, the Aesir noticed the shape of the net in the smouldering ashes and recognized its value, so quickly made one for themselves. They threw the net into the waterfall. Thor held one end and all the other Aesir held the other, and together they dragged the net through the water. But Loki swam along in front of them, then squeezed himself between two stones on the riverbed so that he was unreachable. Then the gods weighted the net so that nothing could pass beneath it. Once again Loki swam before the net, but realizing that he would soon be in the open sea, he leapt over the net and swam back to the waterfall.

The Aesir made a third attempt to drag the river, and this time Thor waded behind the net. Loki now faced two alternatives: the mortal danger of entering the sea or the equal danger of confronting Thor. He decided to leap as quickly as he could over the net, but Thor caught him by the tail, which explains why the salmon tapers at its rear.

The gods were determined to punish Loki for his part in Balder's death. He was bound with his own son's entrails, as shown on this stone cross from Cumbria in England.

The Aesir were not about to forgive Loki: he was dragged to a dark cave where they set three stone slabs on edge. Loki's son, Vali, was transformed into a wolf and Loki was forced to watch him tear his other son, Narfi, to pieces. Then the Aesir used Narfi's intestines to bind Loki across the three stones. Skadi took a poisonous snake and fixed it over Loki's head so that venom dripped onto his face. Loki's wife Sigyn stood beside him with a bowl to catch the poison, but when it had filled up she had to empty it. To escape the venomous drops again, Loki wrenched away so hard that he caused an earthquake. And there he is destined to lie until he breaks free at Ragnarok.

The Funeral of a God

All the Aesir were filled with grief at the demise of their beloved Balder, and so they gave him a magnificent funeral. The god was placed on his ship and it was launched, engulfed in flames, into the sea. In Viking times, this funerary custom was reserved for the elite – kings, princes or other affluent and favoured members of the community.

Beings of many kinds attended Balder's cremation: Odin with his ravens, Frigg, with all the Valkyries, Freyr in his chariot drawn by the golden boar Gullinbursti, Freyja with her cats, and Heimdall on his horse, Gulltopp. A great throng of frost-giants and mountain-giants were also present, together with elves, dwarves and the rest of the gods.

The Aesir were unable to launch Balder's ship, Hringhorni, the biggest one of all, so they had to summon a giantess named Hyrrokkin. She arrived from Jotunheim riding in a chariot drawn by a vicious wolf, using poisonous snakes for reins to guide her steed.

Hyrrokkin pushed the boat out with just a nudge while flames flew from the rollers and the earth quaked. Thor was so angry at being unable to acomplish the task himself that he raised his hammer to smash the giantess's skull. But the other gods begged for mercy on her behalf, and eventually placated him.

As Balder's body was carried on to the ship, his wife Nanna collapsed and died from grief, and was laid next to him on the pyre. Then the Aesir set the ship alight and Thor consecrated it with his hammer, Mjollnir. At the same time, an unfortunate dwarf named Lit happened to run in front of Thor's foot. The god kicked him onto the burning ship, where he perished.

The giantess Hyrrokkin, who arrived in a chariot drawn by a wolf, was invited by the gods to push Balder's funeral ship into the ocean.

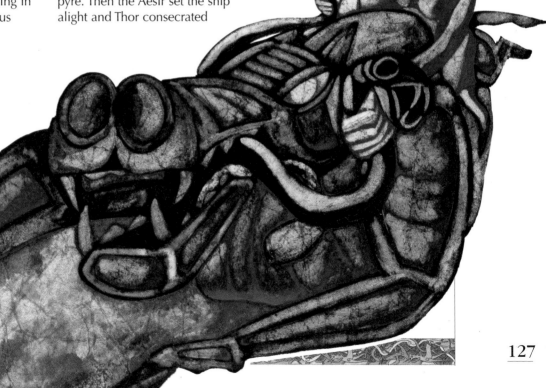

The End of the World

The idea of fate infused Norse mythology; destiny was immutable. This concept culminated in Ragnarok, the coming destruction of the world whose inevitability was felt throughout Norse mythology. So precisely was it preordained that the details of what would happen were already known, and the gods prepared for it daily. But even though Ragnarok meant universal disorder, annihilation would not be total.

The word Ragnarok is a compound: the first element, *ragna*, means "organizing powers" and was commonly used to refer to the gods. The second, *rok*, means "fate" or "destiny". Thus the term as a whole meant the fate or destiny of the gods. The second element became confused, however, quite early in the study of Germanic mythology, with *rokkr*, meaning "twilight", giving rise to the title of the conclusive opera in Wagner's *Ring* cycle, *Götterdämmerung*, "Twilight of the Gods".

Although it was to bring about their destruction, the gods could not halt the onset of Ragnarok. It had to come to pass as prophesied, and all they could do was show stoic bravery in the face of certain destruction. To the Norse people, fate was a fact of life, something that could not in any way be avoided or changed, and had to be met without fear. Even death, the ultimate end, was already decreed and needed to be encountered with brave acceptance. To laugh in the face of death was one of the greatest achievements that a Norse warrior could perform, and such a warrior was long remembered by his peers.

Ragnarok was described in the *Eddas* in imagery that, like the creation myths, appears to have been influenced by the natural phenomena of Iceland. The world was to be destroyed by fire and water, with steam and flames rising to the skies – a vision which could well have been inspired by the experience of volcanic eruptions.

The Norse people imagined the end of the world in terms of the coming together of fire and water – a combination that may have been suggested by volcanic activity surrounding geysers such as this one in Langarvatn, western Iceland.

Heimdall the Horn Blower

Heimdall was a particularly enigmatic figure in the Norse pantheon, so much so that it is not certain whether he was a member of the Aesir or the Vanir. He was the watchman of the gods, and the blowing of his trumpet, Gjallarhorn ("Resounding Horn"), which could be heard across the three levels of the universe, would sound the onset of Ragnarok.

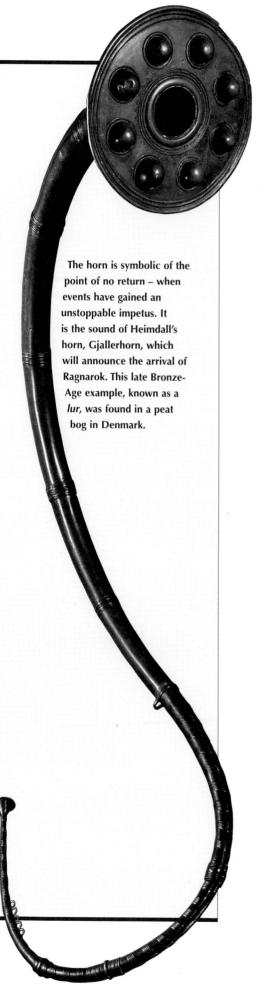

The horn is symbolic of the point of no return – when events have gained an unstoppable impetus. It is the sound of Heimdall's horn, Gjallerhorn, which will announce the arrival of Ragnarok. This late Bronze-Age example, known as a *lur*, was found in a peat bog in Denmark.

Heimdall's origin was unusual; he was said to be the son of nine sisters who all gave birth to him simultaneously. In some sources these nine maidens were identified as giantesses, while elsewhere they were associated with the waves of the sea, believed to be the nine daughters of Aegir.

According to Snorri, Heimdall was called the "white god" and was held to be very great and holy. He was also known as Gullintanni "Golden-toothed" and Hallinskidi (possibly meaning "One with Leaning Sticks", but used poetically to refer to a ram). His horse was named Gulltopp ("golden top").

Heimdall dwelt in the hall called Himinbjorg, beside the bridge Bifrost that connected Asgard with Midgard. His role was to sit at the border of Asgard every day guarding the bridge against attempted crossings by giants. Heimdall was well suited to his position as watchman because he possessed marvellous eyesight: he could see for a distance of one hundred leagues, equally as well by night as by day. His hearing was just as extraordinary: he could hear grass springing from the ground or wool growing on sheep. He was also ever-wakeful, and needed less sleep than a bird. These qualities were essential to the gods because he was alert to the events that would mark the onset of Ragnarok, which could occur at any time. At its first signs Heimdall was expected to raise Gjallarhorn aloft and sound it, signalling to the gods to prepare for the last great battle.

Heimdall was the mortal enemy of Loki, just as the Midgard serpent was the particular enemy of Thor. Loki and Heimdall were destined to fight one-to-one and destroy each other during Ragnarok, but an earlier conflict between them is also described in a myth. Taking the shape of seals, the two gods fought over a beautiful "sea-kidney" which Snorri identified as the Necklace of the Brisings. From this story it could be deduced that Heimdall may have been a shape-changer.

Heimdall was also said to be the progenitor of the different classes of men (see page 118), and the seeress-narrator of *Voluspa* refered to men as the sons of Heimdall. It is not clear why Heimdall rather than the all-father, Odin, should have been considered the begetter of human society, but the claims made for him in this respect at least attest to his importance in the pantheon, even if we know little else about him.

Descriptions of major eruptions bear a marked resemblance to the sequence of events during Ragnarok; mountains are shaken by earthquakes, the sun disappears due to the clouds of smoke, and ash, flames, smoke and steam fill the sky. Melting ice can cause floods of water to run alongside rivers of burning lava. The long Icelandic winter must also have helped shape the vision of Ragnarok's summerless years.

The Vision of the Apocalypse

Snorri describes the events of Ragnarok in great detail. First, he claims, fierce battles will rage throughout the world for three years. Motivated by greed, brothers will kill each other. No mercy will be shown and the ties of kinship will not even prevent fathers from killing their sons.

A terrible winter will prevail, called Fimbulwinter; snow will drift from all directions and great frosts will cover the land. Biting winds will be constant and the sun will fail to shine. Three such winters will follow with no summer in between. The wolf chasing the sun will finally swallow it, to everyone's horror. A second wolf will catch the moon, and that will be equally disastrous.

There will be a huge earthquake – trees will be uprooted, mountains will crash to the ground, and all fetters will break. At the same time both the wolf Fenrir and Loki will be loosened from their bonds. The Midgard serpent will fly into a giant rage and make its way to shore, causing the ocean to surge over the land.

The ship Naglfar, made from dead men's nailclippings, will float loose from its moorings. (It was important that no one in the Viking world

Left: Although during Ragnarok a huge earthquake will cause devastation and all other trees will be uprooted, the World Tree, shown here in a medieval manuscript, will remain standing.

Right: In the final battle, Surt will carry his flaming sword aloft, burning everything around him. A ship bearing Loki and the giants will arrive on the shores of Midgard and the Midgard serpent will rise up from the sea.

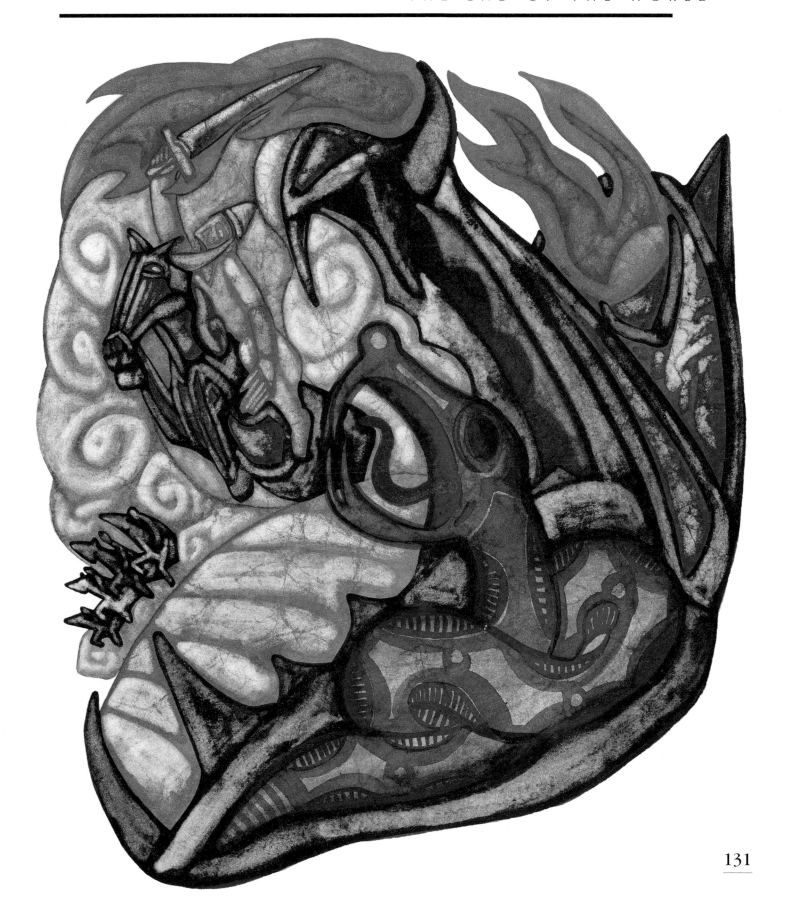

should die with untrimmed nails, for those who did contributed greatly to the construction of this ship, and both gods and men hoped to defer its completion for as long as possible.) Laden with giants, Naglfar will be carried along in the flood of the surging ocean, with Loki at the helm and a giant called Hrym as its captain.

Fenrir will advance with his mouth gaping so wide that his upper jaw will rest against the sky and his lower jaw against the earth – it would gape even wider if there were more room. Flames will flare out from his eyes and nostrils. To one side of him will be the Midgard serpent, which will spit so much poison that it will bespatter the sky and the sea. In all this turmoil the sky will open and from it will ride the sons of Muspell. Surt, who has been stationed throughout time at the frontier of Muspell, will ride at the head of the group brandishing his flaming sword, which will shine

brighter than the sun. Everything around him will be burned. As Muspell's sons ride over Bifrost into Asgard the bridge will break under their weight. They will advance to Vigrid, a plain stretching a hundred leagues in each direction where the last battle will take place. Fenrir will also arrive there, as will the Midgard serpent, and Loki accompanied by Hrym and the frost-giants.

When all this happens, Heimdall will stand up and blow mightily on Gjallarhorn, to awaken all the gods. They will hold counsel together. Odin will ride to Mimir's well and consult Mimir on his own and his people's behalf. The ash Yggdrasill will shake, and nothing in heaven or on earth will be without fear. The Aesir will put on their armour and take up their weapons, and so will all the Einherjar, and they will advance onto Vigrid.

Odin will ride in front wearing a golden helmet and a beautiful mail-coat, carrying his spear,

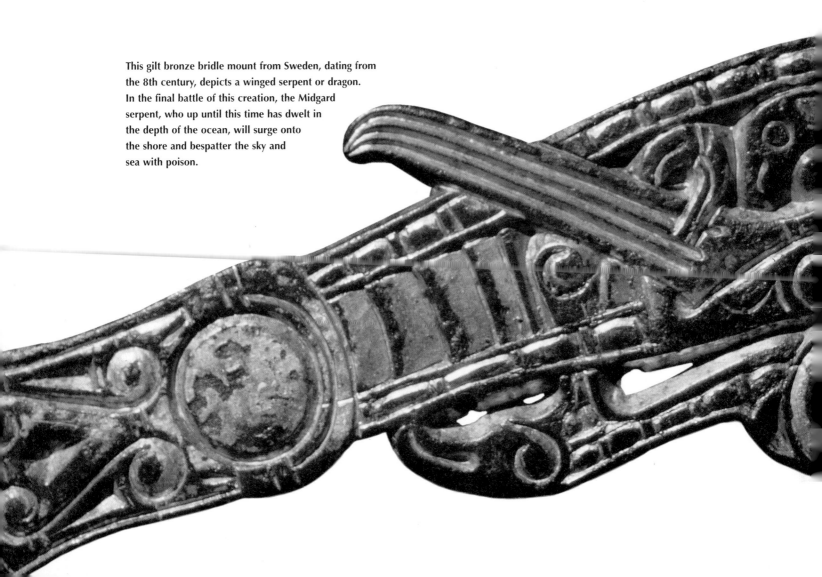

This gilt bronze bridle mount from Sweden, dating from the 8th century, depicts a winged serpent or dragon. In the final battle of this creation, the Midgard serpent, who up until this time has dwelt in the depth of the ocean, will surge onto the shore and bespatter the sky and sea with poison.

Gungnir. He will choose as his foe the wolf Fenrir. Thor will advance at his side but will be unable to help him for he will have his hands full fighting the Midgard serpent. Freyr will battle with Surt for a great length of time, but will eventually succumb because he lacks the good sword that he gave to Skirnir (see page 64).

The snarling hound Garm, an evil creature, will also become free. He will battle with Tyr, and they will struggle to the bitter end. Meanwhile, Thor will vanquish the Midgard serpent, but will retreat only nine paces before he is mortally wounded by its deadly venom. Fenrir will swallow Odin, killing him. But immediately Odin's son Vidar will avenge his father, wearing a shoe that has long been prepared for this moment. Throughout time, material for this shoe has been collected from the waste pieces that people cut off their shoes before repairing them, and anyone keen to assist the Aesir in their time of need must make sure that they throw these pieces away rather than keep them for later use. In the final battle, Vidar will put one foot over the wolf's lower jaw, and grasping his upper jaw, he will tear Fenrir apart, killing him.

A 12th-century glazed pottery egg from Sweden intended as a symbol of rebirth.

Loki will battle with Heimdall, and they will both fall. After that Surt will fling fire over the whole earth so that it burns. Flames, smoke and steam will shoot up to the firmament. The sky will turn black and the stars will disappear. The earth will sink into the engulfing sea that will rise up.

When at last the fires have died down and the seas have subsided, the earth, now grown fair and fertile, will rise again from the sea. Crops will sprout unsown and harvests will be abundant. Odin's sons Vidar and Vali will still be alive, and so will Thor's sons Modi and Magni, who will have possession of the hammer, Mjollnir. Balder and Hod will arrive from Hel, and they will all sit on the grass in the place where Asgard had once been and discuss what happened in former times. These gods will rule the world anew and will tell one another tales of the old gods and of Fenrir and the Midgard serpent.

The sun will also have begotten a daughter, no less fair than herself, just before she was swallowed by the wolf, and the daughter will follow the path of her mother, wending her life-giving way across the sky. The human world will be repopulated by two people, called Lif and Lifthrasir, who will have remained hidden in the ash tree Yggdrasill throughout Ragnarok. Thus the end will contain the germ of a new beginning, and the cycle will start again.

133

THE NORDIC LEGACY

When a religion dies, its legacy can be twofold. At one level, folk beliefs and customs preserve some fragments of the past which are handed on in unbroken tradition with little awareness of their origins owing to the instinctive respect rural communities feel for the ways of earlier generations. The second level, in contrast, is the creation of academic interest. This occurs when scholars, writers and artists of a far later period rediscover the pre-Christian roots of their nation's culture, and consciously use them to pursue a political or artistic agenda. Germanic paganism has left its legacy in both these ways.

By the year AD1000, the work of Christian missionaries, which had begun in Germany some 400 years previously, had penetrated even the remotest areas of Scandinavia. Everywhere the ruling classes had accepted the new faith, and paganism was officially abandoned, although common sense suggests that the conversion was not so sudden or complete as medieval writers claimed.

Nonetheless, pagan worship was condemned, and Christian writers adopted various ways of diminishing its power. To Snorri, although they were wise and powerful, the gods were based on human kings whom pagan men thought to be divine; to others, they were demons or else mere lifeless statues. But their names were never forgotten; not only are four English weekdays named after them, but Germanic and Scandinavian languages are rich in personal names alluding to gods, to heroes, to Valkyries, and to animals, such as the wolf, that had mythical associations.

The personalities of the gods were largely forgotten or distorted; Odin survived only as a leader of the Wild Hunt in a few regions of Sweden, and Freyja was presented as the witch who led the Sabbath orgies on *Walpurgisnacht* (April 30) in German legend. Thor's role as destroyer of giants is reflected in the widespread Scandinavian folk belief that thunderbolts kill trolls and all other harmful goblins and ogres; it is probably also significant that Thursday, Thor's day, is often mentioned in folklore as the best day for carrying out magical procedures, while patterns associated with him, such as the swastika, were called "Thor's Hammer" in Iceland.

So few details are known about the seasonal festivals of pagan times that it is impossible to be

A modern sculpture in Rogaland, Norway, shows three swords embedded in rock. It was inspired by the Nordic legend of the Volsungs (see pages 90–93).

sure whether, for example, the Scandinavian mid-summer bonfires or the German Christmas tree are descended from them, but it seems likely. Another probable pagan survival is the notion that at mid-winter elves, trolls, and other such supernatural beings try to invade human houses to hold their own destructive revels there. This links with the winter custom of men dressing themselves in grotesque disguises (such as animal masks, horned masks and costumes made of straw or skins) and going from house to house to bring good luck and receive food and drink. Finally, there is the mid-winter gift-bringer, whose female forms (Perchta, Holde or Mother Holla) show clear similarities to Germanic goddesses; the male form, whom we know as Santa Claus, is basically Christian, but has recently acquired, at least in Scandinavia and America, a retinue of cheerful pagan elves to replace the little black demon who, in European tradition, once accompanied him to punish naughty children.

It is the minor supernatural beings – giants, trolls, elves, dragons and goblins of every sort – who survived virtually unchanged from paganism into the fairy stories of recent times. In folklore, as in the pre-Christian records, there are quarrelsome giants, dwarf miners and smiths, seductive fairy women, ogres and goblins, monsters, swan maidens, mermen, werewolves, shape-changers and witches. It would of course be wrong to consider all this rich material solely as a legacy from Germanic paganism. Much of it can be matched in the folk tales of Celtic and Slavonic lands, so it is more accurate to talk of a basic European repertoire of pre-Christian concepts adapted to varying local conditions than to draw sharp national or linguistic boundaries. Nevertheless, the parallels between past paganism and modern Germanic folklore which Jakob Grimm (the more scholarly of the two famous brothers) set out in his *Deutsche Mythologie* (1835) remain valid and enlightening.

One interesting continuity concerns the concept of death. Archaeology and written sources both show that in pagan times it was widely held that the dead "lived" inside their own graves or

A modern re-enactment of Ragnarok. Masks such as these, depicting elves, dwarves and trolls, are also worn for the midwinter custom of visiting homes to bring good fortune.

burial mounds, from which they might emerge as physical "undead". In more recent Germanic folk-lore, the Christian concept of a ghost as the bodi-less manifestation of the soul of the dead is indeed common, but alongside it is a strong survival of the pagan belief in the "walking dead". Nineteenth-century Iceland had the powerfully physical *draugur*, and also "the sending", which is a dead man raised from his grave by a wizard to perform tasks at his command; Germany had the *Nachzehrer*, a corpse which lives on in the grave, chewing its own limbs, and which may emerge to attack the living; Danish ghosts, though spirits rather than corpses, are often said to be laid by being staked or imprisoned under a stone, just as was done to bog bodies many centuries before.

Scholarly interest in ancient myths and hero tales began with the discovery of the *Poetic Edda* in Iceland in 1640, and spread rapidly throughout the seventeenth and eighteenth centuries as translations of Eddic poems, heroic sagas, and the works of Saxo and Snorri appeared in other Scandinavian languages, in German and English, and even in French. This led to a lively debate as to the relative value of Nordic and Greek myths in art and education; in Germany, for instance, Herder saw Nordic myths as noble, but Schiller

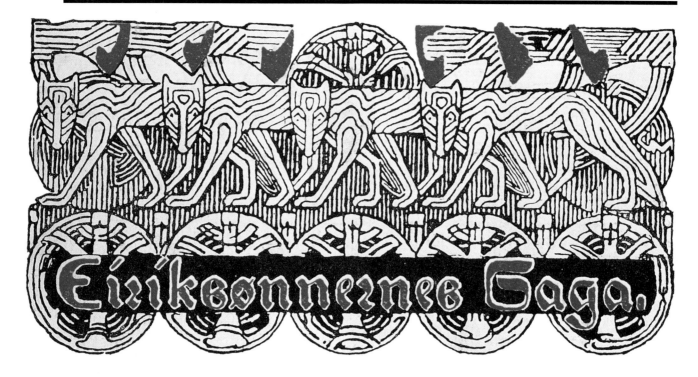

A 20th-century illustration for a retelling of the saga of Eric the Red by Gerhard Munthe which uses the wolf – an animal common in Germanic legends – as its motif.

thought them too plain and down-to-earth to inspire a poet. Most writers and painters in Scandinavia had no such doubts; there, nineteenth-century Romanticism was full of nostalgic admiration for the heroic age, revelling in ancient grave-mounds, warriors in winged or horned helmets, dragon ships, runestones, temples, bards, Valkyries, gods and goddesses.

Nostalgia for past glories often had patriotic and political implications. When the Danish navy held off the English attack on Copenhagen in 1801, poets described the ancient kings emerging from their burial mounds, led by Thor, to inspire their descendants, and Valhalla opening to welcome Villemoes, a famous naval officer killed in this war. Political conflict both within and between Denmark and Germany, could be expressed through similar images; for Wagner, Siegfried symbolized not only courage and nobility, but also liberation from economic oppression; in the 1930s, left-wing German workers' movements were interested in the old myths; in the 1940s, a Danish newspaper conveyed hostility to the German occupation by retelling two heroic legends from Saxo. The Nazi stress on Germanic racial nobility, and on its pagan heritage, is only one instance (although

notorious) of a widespread tendency to politicize mythology. Some Nazis even wished to reinstate the public worship of Wotan (Odin) and Thor, but Hitler thought the attempt would be foolish, and it was not carried out.

Creative writers soon began reworking myths and hero legends in prose, poetry and drama. A striking example is Leconte de Lisle's *Poèmes barbares* (1862), which includes poems based on Nordic texts. In one, a Valkyrie urges her dead father in his grave-mound to give her his sword, threatening to call wolves to scatter his bones if he refuses; in another, a dying hero asks a raven to tear the heart from his breast and take it to his beloved; a third is a passionate account of the deaths of Sigurd and Brynhild. Strindberg uses a comic *Edda* poem in which Loki insults all the other gods as a model for his own poem *Lokes Smädelser* (1884), a satire on the assassinations of certain European statesmen.

By far the greatest of these creative reworkings is Richard Wagner's libretto for his cycle of four operas, *The Ring of the Nibelungs* (1852). Despite its title, which echoes that of the famous medieval German poem, Wagner's script owes far more to the Icelandic texts about the Volsungs. He tightened the plot by various devices of his own, notably by transferring the incest theme from Sinfjotli's birth to that of Siegfried (Sigurd), and involving Brynhild (Brunhilde) in the tragedy of Siegmund and Sieglinde (Signy). He greatly increased the role of the gods, and gave the whole drama a cosmic dimension by linking Siegfried's fate and the curse on the treasure to the ultimate destruction of the gods; this does not occur anywhere in the various original sources. At a deeper level, he filled the story with his personal philosophical and political ideas, so that Siegfried represents the freedom-loving ideals of the 1848 revolutionaries and his own opposition to capitalist values. Wagner's widow and sons, unfortunately, preferred to stress the theme of racial purity, undeniably present in the cycle; it thus acquired the reputation of a proto-Nazi work, from which it took time to recover.

English literature contains two large-scale reworkings of Nordic material. The first, William Morris's poem *The Story of Sigurd the Volsung* (1862), is now virtually forgotten; it retells Sigurd's tragedy in leisurely, detailed style and is often moving, but with nostalgic pathos rather than the curt ferocity of the older sources. Second, and far more influential, is the work of J. R. R. Tolkien, a scholar steeped in Nordic and Anglo-Saxon traditions, from which he evolved his personal mythology. *The Hobbit* and *The Lord of the Rings* both draw copiously on Scandinavian myth and magic; through Tolkien and his imitators, this tradition has now re-entered the mainstream of fantasy fiction.

Finally, mention should be made of the conscious revival of paganism since the 1970s. Neo-Pagans combine features from many periods and places, often showing a preference for Celtic material; however, there are groups specializing in Germanic/Scandinavian paganism – the Odinic Rite in Britain, Asatru groups in Iceland, and the Nordic Pagan Federation in Norway. The legacy of the North still manifests itself in unexpected ways.

Odin holds his sword aloft in a 1976 stage production of Wagner's *The Valkyrie* (*Die Walküre*) by the San Francisco Opera. Wagner's *Ring of the Nibelungs*, of which this opera is a part, has been scrutinized for a racial message, but has always retained its popularity.

Glossary of Gods and Key Characters

This glossary contains names of the principal Norse gods and characters in Norse and Germanic mythology. Old Norse names have been simplified.

Aegir the sea god who dwelt in the depths of the ocean where he often held banquets for the gods.

Etzel a Germanic hero based on the real-life Attila the Hun.

Fenrir the wolf bound by the Aesir that broke free and battled against them during Ragnarok. He was one of Loki's three pernicious offspring.

Freyja the fertility goddess who exchanged sexual favours with four dwarves to win for herself the Necklace of the Brisings that they had forged from gold. She adored riches and was said to weep tears of gold for her absent husband Od.

Frigg Odin's wife and queen of the Aesir. Her sons included Balder and Hod. She was invoked by women during childbirth and by those wishing to conceive.

Gerd the daughter of giants whose name was linked to the Norse word for field. She was married to Freyr.

Hel the monstrous daughter of Loki who presided over the citadel (of the same name) in Niflheim, where those who did not die in battle were destined to go.

Jormungand also known as the Midgard Serpent. Another of Loki's evil children, he was to writhe up onto land spurting forth poison and attack the gods in the final battle.

Loki the trickster companion of the Norse gods whose influence gradually became malevolent. He eventually caused the death of Balder, precipitating Ragnarok, the apocalypse, in which he sided with the giants against the gods.

Nerthus an enigmatic earth goddess who may have been one of a divine pair with Njord, god of the sea.

Njord a god of the Vanir who ruled the wind and controlled the bounty of the ocean.

Odin the Norse and Germanic god also known as Wotan and Woden. He was the primary god of the Aesir.

Siegfried (also known as Sigurd) a Germanic hero in both the Volsung and Nibelung legends.

Sif the beautiful golden-haired goddess who was married to Thor. Loki mischievously cut her hair off and then sought assistance from the dwarves, who made her a new head of hair.

Skadi a mountain goddess who was offered a choice of husband from among the unmarried Aesir. She was only allowed to see their feet before making her choice.

Sleipnir Odin's eight-legged magical horse, born to Loki after he took the shape of a mare.

Thor the huge god of the Aesir who ruled over thunder. He carried a hammer, Mjollinir, and used it to protect the pantheon.

Valkyrie female spirits thought to be immortal who went down to battlefields both to grant victory according to Odin's decree and to lead the slain warriors back to Asgard. There they waited upon the heroes, serving them food, singing and dancing.

Yggdrasill the World Tree. It formed the axis of the universe and all that lived in it.

Index

Further Reading

Batey, C., Clarke, H., Page, R. I. and Price, N. S., *Cultural Atlas of the Viking World*. Time-Life Books, Amsterdam, 1994.

Crossley-Holland, K., *The Penguin Book of Norse Myths: Gods of the Vikings*. Penguin, London, 1980.

Davidson, H. R. Ellis, *Gods and the Myths of Northern Europe*. Penguin, Harmondsworth, 1964.

Davidson, H. R. Ellis, *Pagan Scandinavia*. Hamlyn, London, 1984.

Davidson, H. R. Ellis, *Lost Beliefs of Northern Europe*. Routledge, London, 1993.

Magnusson, M., *Viking: Hammer of the North*. Orbis, London, 1976.

Owen, G. R., *Rites and Religions of the Anglo-Saxons*. David and Charles, Newton Abbot, 1981.

Page, R. I., *Chronicles of the Vikings*. British Museum Press, London, 1995.

Page, R. I., *Norse Myths*. British Museum Press, London, 1993.

Simek, R., *Dictionary of Northern Mythology*. Boydell and Brewer, Woodbridge, 1993.

Todd, M., *The Early Germans*. Blackwell, Oxford, 1992.

Turville-Petre, E. O. G., *Myth and Religion of the North*. Weidenfeld, London, 1964.

Picture Credits